The Levitan Pitch.
Buy This Book.
Win More Pitches.

Peter Levitan

Portlandia Press
Portland

The Levitan Pitch. Buy This Book. Win More Pitches.

ISBN: 978-0-9883119-2-3

Portlandia Press
Portland, Oregon

This book is dedicated to the memory of Michael Keeshan.

No one was smarter or funnier.

The Levitan Pitch.

CHAPTER 3 WHAT CLIENTS WANT

CHAPTER 4 TEACHABLE MOMENTS

CHAPTER 5 THE LEVITAN PITCH SYSTEM

CHAPTER 7 THE FRONTLINES

CONCLUSION

APPENDICES

ACKNOWLEDGMENTS

ABOUT THE AUTHOR

"I tell the kids, somebody's gotta win, somebody's gotta lose. Just don't fight about it. Just try to get better."

Yogi Berra

INTRODUCTION

A Quick, Painful, Admission

This book is riddled with critical mistakes.

These mistakes are made every day by advertising, design, digital, and PR agencies across the globe. Unfortunately, these mistakes negatively impact one of the most important things in the life of a marketing services agency... winning new business.

How do I know about these mistakes? I've talked with dozens of agency managers and owners, B2C and B2B clients, leading pitch consultants, procurement executives, and the most unfortunate information source of all... my own advertising career.

I've pitched large multinational corporations and small local clients. I've worked at Dancer Fitzgerald Sample, at the time New York's largest agency, at Saatchi & Saatchi Advertising Worldwide, founded two Internet start-ups, and was the owner of a two-office advertising and design agency in Oregon.

I've worked with experienced agency search consultants and inexperienced clients who were running their first agency pitch. I've travelled to pitch in Frankfurt, Seoul, and Oshkosh for multinational accounts and pitched the local hospital, bank, and restaurant in my own conference room. I've run pitches as the business development director of the world's largest agency, as the CEO of a small one, and I have even been pitched to by agencies when I worked the client side.

Based on 30 years of sitting on both sides of the table, I know that there is no such thing as a standard marketing services pitch scenario. Every client category, assignment, timetable, budget, search consultant, procurement system, and client personality is unique. There are times when a pitch for a major account is handled efficiently and times when a pitch for a short-term assignment is an absurdly complicated and drawn out affair.

However...

While there is no standard pitch or agency, I know from experience that there are universal pitch criteria that can be identified and addressed regardless of the type or size of client, specific marketing objectives, or agency. To that extent, *The Levitan Pitch* is designed to deliver one master benefit:

You will win more new clients.

It's that simple. Given the very high cost of writing, planning, and running a business development program, responding to RFI's and RFP's, crafting compensation proposals, attending client chemistry meetings, and creating and running a finalist presentation, there is no doubt that your organization will benefit from having a dedicated pitch management system.

———

In Chapter One of this book, I discuss the very high cost of failing to run well-crafted, efficient pitches. The costs of failure include poor agency staff morale, individual employee burnout, and the financial cost to an agency's bottom-line that comes from the cost of participating in four-month agency searches and funding an agency's annual business development plan. There can also be significant costs to career advancement, as you will see from my personal experience in my story about "The Worst Advertising Pitch Ever".

Chapter Two offers an escape hatch. You should not pitch every account that comes knocking. I give you a handy tool to gauge both the value of the prospective client and your agency's chances of winning. This is a rather good exercise to do before you embark on the path of winding up the agency to build your finalist pitch.

Chapter Three begins to help you position the pitch for success. We look at the essential facts of the pitch and dig into understanding the client's mindset by understanding the type of assignment, type of relationship they are looking for, and what type of agency will fulfill their needs.

Chapter Four delivers my list of "*The 12 Deadliest Presentation Mistakes*". These are identified pitch killers that come from my personal experience and the experiences of agency CEO's, clients, and search consultants. The accompanying cartoons wouldn't be as funny if these mistakes were not being made over and over, even by the most sophisticated agencies.

In Chapter Five I lay out thirty short but very sweet suggestions for how to build a brilliant presentation that I know will greatly increase your odds of winning. These ideas cover three core elements of a successful pitch: process management, content development, and how to deliver a standout presentation. Each rule is supported by a tip or insight that offers a fast way to achieve your objectives. One of my favorite insights is how to use LinkedIn recommendations to understand the personalities and interests of the clients that will be in the presentation. This insight isn't what you think.

Chapter Six is all about *don't take my word for it*. This chapter brings in valuable learning via fourteen interviews with a range of communications industry experts. It is informative and often mind-blowing to hear the pitch related experiences and advice of agency search consultants, compensation experts, an ex P&G procurement executive, a negotiation trainer, the 4A's, the Association of National Advertisers, a silicon valley presentation guru, a leading agency strategist, an ex-Nike and W+K executive on building chemistry, an IP lawyer on who actually owns *your* pitch ideas, the CEO of a London advertising agency, and the CEO of an independent agency network who has been on both sides of the table.

Finally, I've included insights about all too common agency pitch mistakes from 16 of the world's leading search consultants.

―――――

I hope that you will find the book informative, insightful, occasionally humorous, and most importantly, a good read that ultimately results in more wins for your company.

I've written this book for "advertising" agencies. However, when I say advertising agency, I really mean all marketing communications agencies including design, digital, social media, and PR agencies. We all run similar business development programs with similar pitch dynamics.

In fact, I think that this book has value for anyone who is selling in today's business marketplace. As Daniel H. Pink says in his book *To Sell Is Human*, "Whether we're employees pitching colleagues a new idea, entrepreneurs enticing funders, or parents and teachers cajoling children to study, we spend our days trying to move others. Like it or not, we are all in sales now."

If you are unfamiliar with advertising lingo, here is a quick guide to the most common acronyms used throughout this book.

4A's: American Association of Advertising Agencies
ANA: Association of National Advertisers
AOR: Agency Of Record
CMO: Chief Marketing Officer
CRM: Customer Relationship Management
ECD: Executive Creative Director
RFI: Request For Information
RFP: Request For Proposal
ROI: Return On Investment
P&L: Profit and Loss

CHAPTER **1**

THE GOOD, BAD AND UGLY

Congratulations!

You are holding a copy of *The Levitan Pitch* in your hands, so the chances are pretty good that you will soon be helping to lead your agency team into a new business pitch.

Getting into a pitch is a good thing. Winning it is much better.

Let's face it: pitching for any new business account is a stressful process. You have to marshal your agency's best and brightest while juggling your existing clients and limited, often stretched resources. This is a particularly painful process for small to mid-sized agencies that are already working at warp speed and may have had back-to-back RFP submissions and pitches. It is no surprise that the stress of pitching can reduce your team's effectiveness.

Research with agency employees supports this proposition.

47%!

A December 2013 research study of advertising professionals by Provoke Insights supports the idea that agency employees are dissatisfied with their agency's pitch process.

> *"Approximately half (47% of respondents) of advertising professionals surveyed by Provoke Insights say they are dissatisfied with the current internal approach to pitching."*

Other issues include:

> *"unrealistic timelines" (66%) and "long work hours" (65%.)*

I've run new client pitches across the Saatchi & Saatchi Advertising Worldwide network and at my own agency. There are few things that we can do in our industry that are as exciting as pitching for that perfect client.

Unfortunately, as you can see from this agency pitch research, it sure doesn't look like many agencies are running efficient pitches. Starting pitches with half of agency employees dreading the pitch process is not a good starting point. High anxiety places your agency a couple of paces back before you have even stepped into the batting box.

How to create and run an efficient *and* successful pitch is exactly what this book is all about.

More Painful Math

Advertising agency pitches are expensive.

Agency CEO's and Business Development Directors occasionally use metaphors to help describe their business development efforts. One of the all-time favorites is how similar agencies are to cobblers and shoes. Cobblers do not have the time to make shoes for their children, and too many agencies don't make the time to run smart business development programs.

Here's another metaphor.

Agencies (OK, American agencies) often point to the career batting averages of major league baseball players when they discuss the success rate of their new business programs. As they put it, even baseball Hall of Famers are perceived as victorious if they have a career batting average of .300 or more. That's only 3 hits for every 10 times at bat. Even the great Hall of Famer Reggie Jackson only had a .261 batting average. In agency think, this would mean that the agency would be Hall of Fame material if they won 3 out of every 10 pitches.

Let's do some agency math using the 1:3 ratio.

Based on my personal experience, conversations with agency CEO's, and a review of existing data, on average, small to medium agency responds to 10 RFP's and participates in 6 pitches per year. Your mileage may vary but let's go with this.

My estimated cost per RFP is $15,000 based on 150 hours of work at a direct labor cost of $100 per hour. At ten RFP's per year, that's a participation cost of $150,000 per year.

A conservative estimate of an average finalist pitch, which includes external and internal meetings, pitch management, strategic planning, writing, creative work, pitch design (as in leave-behinds and supporting digital programs), the pitch itself, T&E, and post presentation follow-up costs an agency approximately $35,000. If an agency does 6 pitches per year that's $210,000.

Obviously, given the size range between multinational networks and small shops, an agency's mileage may vary but these numbers seem fair for the average agency, and they help frame the issue.

Using my scenario, the total annual cost for RFP's and pitching comes to $360,000. This number does not include the day-to-day costs of business development. If you add in management, creative, analog and digital marketing, and business development director time, an agency could easily top out at over $500,000 in labor and outsourced business development costs per year. I am ball-parking here just to get to a reference number.

It can get much more costly. The search consultant David Wethey of Agency Assessments International reports that the average pitch cost per

UK agency was £178,000 in 2010. Channeling Las Vegas, as an agency owner I've put my own hard earned cash on the line to win new business. As I write this book, Microsoft just handed their international account to Interpublic. Just imagine how much it took to win that pitch.

Bottom line… an agency could easily spend $500,000 to have a "Hall of Fame" business development batting average of .300. Given today's decreasing creative services industry profit margins, these numbers could be considered depressing.

Do you like this math? I don't.

The purpose of *The Levitan Pitch* is to help you dramatically improve your agency's business development batting average by improving the effectiveness and efficiency of how you manage and run new business pitches. I believe that this will increase your success rate and importantly, your ROI.

You will do that by being both more mental *and* more physical. Thank you Yogi for pointing the way.

The Levitan Pitch Playbook

"Baseball is ninety percent mental and the other half is physical."

- Yogi Berra

I love this famous quote because Yankee Hall Of Famer Yogi Berra is so right. By the time you make it to the majors, i.e. the opportunity to pitch for a large account that might change the direction and fortunes of your agency, you've done some serious mental work, and now it's time get physical.

You are holding my 'mental' book. The objective of this book is to provide you, as a pitch leader, with a range of odds-increasing insights on how to manage a new business pitch. These insights run the gamut from how to make the all-important "should we or shouldn't we pitch" decision (you still have time to recognize that this isn't a pitch you should play in), to critical legal and IP decisions, to compensation and negotiating with procurement, to how you manage the pitch development scenario itself.

The book stands alone, but it is best used in conjunction with the tools I have in the *Levitan Pitch Playbook* that's located on my website at www.peterlevitan.com.

Elements of the *Levitan Pitch Playbook* have been designed as 'physical' management tools that you will share with the individual members of your pitch team. The *Playbook*'s objective is to assist with the daily management of your team and to literally get everyone on the same page, as well as increase the efficiency of your pitch development process.

Use the *Playbook* to get past the inefficiency of the standard pitch process and reduce your agency's collective groan when they hear that you are about to embark on yet another new pitch. I have a list of *Playbook* tools in the Appendix.

Why Are There Groans?

Despite the fact that we all want to be invited to the right pitch for the right client, there are a number of reasons why 47% of your staff might collectively groan at the start of virtually any new pitch. These groans could be related to your agency's current state of mind or existing pitch fatigue and might indicate that there are good reasons to stop right now and ask that super tough question…

"Should we pitch this account?"

This is your chance to dig deep, and start to do a real gut-check before you get in too deep.

Eight Universal Groan Inducers

1. Your agency management is starting to look like it will pitch any client that raises their hand.

2. Your agency team is wondering if it really wants this client. They may have heard that the client is a nightmare, that they are penurious, that they don't respect the creative process, they are fickle, or that the incumbent agency is a lock, and on and on. Whatever…. your mates are getting the wrong vibes.

3. Your agency knows that winning this client is a long shot. Yes, you have been invited to pitch a big one. Yes, the client must like you. Yes, your team is happy. But they also have a bad feeling that this pitch has very low odds of succeeding. Realism has crept in. Agency staff can in fact be objective.

4. You just finished submitting yet another grueling RFP response.

5. You just finished a huge pitch and – won or lost – everyone is exhausted.

6. You just won a new account and should spending your scarce resources to bring them onboard.

7. You don't have a clear pitch process, and your staff is already dreading the prospect of yet another round of 12-hour days.

8. Agency staff recognizes the personal cost of pitching and not winning. They'd like agency management to keep some of that cash to distribute at bonus time.

Read on: I can help you de-groan. As temporary consolation for small to medium size agencies, even global agency networks suffer from groaning.

The Worst Advertising Agency Presentation – Ever

I won my first pitch in 1984. I was an account executive at Dancer, Fitzgerald Sample which at the time was New York's largest "*Mad Men*" era advertising agency (Saatchi & Saatchi bought DFS in 1987). The pitch was for Western Union's $15 million EasyLink Service. EasyLink was the first commercial email service and launched the same year as the IBM PC – the times were changing fast. We won the pitch, and I learned how a well-oiled pitch worked from a new business team that won nine out of ten pitches that year.

After I began working on the business, I asked the senior client why we won. She stated three reasons:

1. We took the time to do the research to understand this brand new market. We arrived with the insight that we needed to lead with the benefit of what we called "Instant Mail" and not the packet-switching story of electronic mail.

2. She was dazzled by our presentation technology. We used a large bank of slide projectors (this was 1984) to deliver our presentation across a huge screen. Remember, the client was a technologist and our presentation tools were perfectly mated to her background.

3. She liked us. The people factor matters.

After that first pitch, my batting average was a sweet 1000.

Not all of my pitches went that smoothly, and over the years I've learned from my winners *and* losers.

Here is the story about the worst, most painful and potentially career-ending advertising agency pitch I've ever been involved in.

Let me warn you that it is a sad – but *instructive* story.

You'll learn about hopes and dreams, pitch management, ego management, client psychology, *and* baby seals.

Saatchi & Saatchi and Adidas

In 1992, Saatchi & Saatchi moved me from New York to London to run business development and the Johnson & Johnson and Sara Lee accounts across Europe and the Middle East. The agency set me up with a sweet ex-pat package that included staff, a nice T&E budget, and a house in Notting Hill.

To say this was a cool move and a big job would be an understatement.

Shortly after I arrived, my London friends moved me into what had been Maurice Saatchi's old office before he and Charles moved across town to the more palatial International HQ building.

To say that sitting at Maurice's old desk was cool would be another understatement.

One day I was in my office with Maurice and Jeremy Sinclair (Saatchi's Global Executive Creative Director), and while discussing the new business program, Maurice turned to Jeremy and said…

*"Boy, we made a lot of bad decisions in **this** office."*

As it turned out, I was about to witness them making more bad decisions.

A few weeks after that meeting, Maurice told me that we were going to pitch the global Adidas account. Huge brand, global business, cool category, big budget, powerful competition, and a potentially great creative platform. Everything an agency could wish for.

At that time, Nike was on its world domination streak, and Adidas had to step up their marketing. Nike wanted to kick Adidas' butt by taking market share from Adidas' global soccer business. Adidas was getting very nervous. And there is nothing like pitching a highly motivated client that knows it has to step up it's marketing.

But, wait – wait, there's more… and it was very personal.

If we won the account, I would open and manage my very own sports marketing agency to run the Adidas account because, Saatchi had an existing sporting goods client conflict in the network.

A couple of days later, Maurice and the reclusive Charles Saatchi and I met with Robert Louis Dreyfus, Adidas' new CEO and majority owner to discuss the pitch. Get this: Robert was a close friend of the agency. He had been the CEO of Saatchi & Saatchi Advertising Worldwide. He was one of us.

One more good thing. Robert asked me to fly from London to Portland, Oregon to meet with Rob Strasser and Peter Moore, who just started running Adidas America. Rob and Peter were sports industry superstars who helped Phil Knight build Nike and were instrumental in the signing of Michael Jordan. Rob and Peter told me that they wanted Saatchi to help lead Adidas marketing into the 90's. Adidas needed some Saatchi stardust.

Let's stop for a second and parse this out:

I am working with Maurice and Charles Saatchi – the most famous advertising men in the world.

They asked me to run a huge pitch for the global Adidas account.

Adidas' CEO is a close friend of the agency, and the management of Adidas America wants us.

If we win the business, I'd build and run my very own Saatchi sports agency. I was already beginning to visualize a reception area adorned with signed World Cup balls. OK, I am getting ahead of myself.

But wait, there's even more good news. During an early meeting, Robert leans over to me and says:

"Peter, you've won this business as long as you don't fuck up the pitch."

I'm thinking, the world's best agency doesn't fuck up. I don't fuck up.

The Pitch

I am now about to tell you how we did, in fact fuck up, and more importantly for you, what I learned.

I think that it is important to point out that this was my first big pitch as

Saatchi & Saatchi London's business development director. I am very happy to say that I've gotten much better at pitching during the past 20 years.

Because Adidas would be such a huge win for the agency, the Saatchi brothers wanted to participate directly in the pitch. A rarity at that stage of their careers.

Because Adidas had so much potential, they wanted me to use the creative talents of Jeremy Sinclair (the agency's global ECD) and Paul Arden, another London creative all-star.

I was now working with Charles, Jeremy and Paul – three of London's most famous creatives.

Looking good right?

Nope…. we started to make a whole set of brand new mistakes right there in Maurice's old office.

Stay with me, there is a lot of learning here.

Mistake #1:

While we all said that it was my pitch to run, I had a room full of owners and very big creative egos (English Creative egos are very large) that were difficult to control and were rather opinionated.

Lesson:

Every pitch needs to establish one leader and manager. Period.

Mistake #2:

My mega-ego creative team was the wrong team for Adidas. They didn't know sports; they didn't want to study the market, and these middle-aged guys did not understand the motivations of the younger sports shoe consumer.

Paul even called Nike "Nīk."

However, despite his mispronunciation, he did have a BIG idea that was in fact, big. The idea was that sport was akin to GOD.

> Sports is a key ingredient in our humanity: it brings out the best in us and it brings the world together.

Through this BIG IDEA, Adidas would own the power of sports itself.

Yes, that's a big idea. Unfortunately…

The Ego-Team decided that we needed a video for the pitch to deliver the big idea to Adidas. Paul went out on his own, wrote the script, and produced the video. On his own.

To illustrate this big idea, the video included metaphorical images of man's inhumanity to man contrasted with the glory of sports. OK, I got it.

Unfortunately, the imagery went a bit over the top to include individual metaphors like baby seals being beaten on the ice contrasted with the beauty of high jumps. Bloody bloody baby seals!

Que – cringes.

To make matters worse, the video didn't have a budget. You try telling Charles Saatchi how much of *his* money he could spend on *his* pitch. The video wound up costing over £30,000.

Lessons:

Build the right team for the pitch. In this case the team was primarily based on seniority, not perfect fit. (Note: we did have a savvy account planner and well-oiled pitch team also working on the pitch.)

Don't lose control of the process.

Establish a budget going in. Stick with it.

Don't give the creative team too much rope.

By the way, just in case you are thinking that I was completely out of my mind, I had asked some of Saatchi London's other award winning creative teams to come up with alternative ideas that we presented along side the bloody seals video. Due to the egos of the Ego-Team, I had to do this on the QT.

Mistake #3:

I couldn't get these guys to rehearse. I rarely got them in the same room at the same time.

Worse, a couple of days before the pitch, Jeremy began to realize that the baby seal video was going to be difficult to present (a rather large understatement) and told me that *I* was going to present all of the creative work.

Lessons:

Assign roles based on expertise not seniority.

Stick to a plan.

Rehearse and rehearse. A lot.

Mistake #4:

We knew Robert Louis Dreyfus very well. But, we didn't know the Adidas marketing executives. They were not part of the decision to seek a new agency. This pitch was CEO-driven.

In fact, we were not even aware that the Adidas marketing group had already started on a new Adidas campaign approach with London's Leagas Delany.

Lessons:

Know which clients will be in the room and understand their motivations. I should have realized that the Adidas marketing team did not want to be in the pitch. We could have managed this. However, we were so enamored by our relationship with the CEO and access to internal Adidas information that we didn't bother to start relationships with the marketing team before the meeting.

We certainly should have known that beating baby seals to death would alienate virtually everyone in the room. Well, my team knew, but we had lost control of that element of the pitch to the Ego-Team by then.

Mistake #5:

This is actually a mistake wrapped up in what is usually a good thing.

Maurice opened the meeting with a story. Sir Maurice is like the Steve Jobs of agency pitching story telling – with the added benefit of an English accent.

We all know that starting with a story is a good thing. However, since we didn't rehearse, we didn't know that Maurice was going to lead with a story, and we weren't at all prepared to follow this particular one.

The story turned out to be an involved dream sequence about how ancient Egypt, Pharaohs, and Adidas were alike. During the story, even I was spacing out on visions of the Sphinx and pyramids.

In addition to spacing out, I didn't know that Maurice was going to hand the meeting over to me immediately after he talked about *my* being in his Egyptian dream. I'm sitting there listening to my very own dream, and then I hear: "Take it Peter."

Lessons:

Here are all of the lessons…

1. Every pitch needs a leader and manager.

2. Never lose control of the process, which should include a timetable and budget.

3. Make sure that every idea presented is based on a smart brand strategy that is developed from a deep understanding of the market and brand. We had done market research, but it didn't directly support the Sport As God creative concept.

4. Know which clients will be in the room, their backgrounds, and their motivations. Understanding "buyer" motivations is the key to sales, and pitching is a sales meeting after all.

5. Assign agency roles based on expertise – not seniority or "hey, its my turn to pitch". Only your best presenters should ever pitch.

6. Don't give the creative team too much rope.

7. Rehearse.

8. Consider starting with a story. The *right* story.

9. Don't show images of bloodied baby seals.

How did it all work out?

As you might suspect… we did not win the Adidas account, and I didn't get my very own Saatchi & Saatchi sports agency with a wall of World Cup soccer balls.

This pitch, a pitch we should have won, quickly became a famous agency fuck-up story. At least everyone knew that I wasn't solely responsible.

On the positive side, I did learn some powerful lessons and went on to win more pitches in London and New York *and* have this great story to tell.

Retribution? Yes.

Adidas has never ever been lauded for its advertising. I am sure that the best creative agency in the world would have helped.

Nike did in fact kick Adidas' global soccer ass.

We got a good laugh when shortly after the pitch, Adidas' marketing team stole Saatchi's very own brilliant tagline, "Nothing Is Impossible" and humorously reused it as "Impossible Is Nothing".

And… twelve years later, my Portland agency Citrus won AOR business from Nike. I finally had my very own sports agency with Nike as a lead client. At that point, I was a bit more mature and didn't bother with the reception room full of balls.

CHAPTER **2**

TO PITCH OR NOT TO PITCH

Just Say No!

Before you embark on a new pitch, you should be asking yourself one extremely important question…

Should we be pitching this account?

I know what you are thinking… Levitan's kidding right? We've made it through the RFI and RFP stages, and now he wants us to ask if we should even be going to the finals?

It's still ok to say "no", and now is the time to take a deep breath and review a go-no-go decision. You are about to spend a great deal of time and money. Are you sure that you should go through the next step? Are your colleague's groans getting louder? Looking in any way ambivalent about the pitch will not help your pitch team feel good about charging into it. Passionless pitches don't win.

Pitch or not is usually one of the most difficult decisions agency management has to make. There is a good chance that you think that you've already answered this question if you participated in an RFP that led to your selection as a short list candidate. I believe that even if you've performed a sound decision making process, now is the time to stop to determine if this potentially expensive pitch is worth the time, effort, and human and cash cost.

Some agencies view pitching as a numbers game. Swing at more pitches, and you'll get hits. Unfortunately, whiffing will drive down your batting average and the agency's profitability. And eat at its soul.

Really, just stop for a second and think this one through. This is the time to dig deep, and ask yourself if you actually have a good chance of winning the account *and*… if this is the kind of client you really want. Is this client qualified to be *your* client?

The Pick Two Decision

As an agency owner, I always cherished four client attributes. Frankly, if I could get just two of these, I'd be happy. Our client Nike delivered all four.

1. **Fame.** Famous clients look great on your client roster, act as poster children for prospective clients that need third-party reassurance that you deliver results, help you woo more talented creatives, and having famous clients will make your mothers proud.

2. **Creative.** You are in the creative services industry because you are creative and want clients who respect creativity. Creativity to me extends beyond just the creative idea into creative media, strategies, consumer insights, and technology. That said, the bottom line for most agencies is that we want to make great advertising programs, and to get there, you need clients that want that too.

3. **Cash.** Fame is nice. Clios are nice. But cash rules. After all, you are in business. In this case, money means having clients that deliver agency profits. No profits = no staff, no creative, no brilliant social media strategies, no awards… no agency.

4. **Nice.** Early in my career, I was given the advice that I should only work with clients who align with my agency's values and share mutual respect. To take it a step further… work with nice people that you like. If I appear to have gone all gooey, I listened, and it was great advice. Life is too short to work with assholes.

The pick two-decision will help you begin to confirm that you should be pitching this client.

But, there are a few more important things to consider and weigh as you make your decision to proceed.

- Does this client need what you have to offer? Is your experience, expertise, or creative product what they really need (or think they need)?

- Do you know the client's agency selection criteria? Do you think you meet it? Are you the right fit? Can your agency really handle this client? Would *you* hire you?

- Has the client clearly stated what they are looking for? Do they sound smart?

- Has the client discussed budgets and their compensation system? They might not want to provide details, but you should have a good perspective on a range and a system. Too many agencies have gone months deep into a pitch only to find out that they can't afford to work with the client.

- What is the client's agency history? Are they perceived as being a good client? Are they loyal or fickle? Burger King has had at least twelve AOR agencies since 1970. Toyota has had one.

- Is your agency so specialized that the client must hire you?

- Is your agency's location a plus or a minus? Specialists can be further away.

- Are you the outlier agency? The one that's simply invited to round out the list?

- Have you met with client management and started a relationship? Are you simpatico? If you haven't met with them, you should insist that you do it now before you get too far down the road. It is in their best interest to want to meet before the big day.

- If the pitch is managed by an agency search consultant, have you begun to understand *their* role, process, and motivations? Do you know them? Are they being straight with you?

- Is the incumbent in the pitch? If so, why do you think that the client might be replacing them? It is possible that the incumbent is a lock because the client is obligated to put the account up for a procurement-driven review on a scheduled basis? Try to figure this out.

- This next question could be the toughest. Is your agency the incumbent, and should *you* bother pitching your client? Ouch. Clearly, this will be a one-off gut-check question that only you can answer. While you are thinking, keep this less than appealing statistic in mind. According to Advertising Age, "*After all, fewer than 10% of incumbent agencies are estimated – by the reckoning of either the 4A's, industry consultants or Ad Age – to hang on to an account at the conclusion of a review process.*" Because of these odds, many agencies have a no-defend policy.

- Finally, does agency management really want this client? Are they psyched? Will they fully support the pitch?

There are a lot of questions to consider before you say – Go. If your analysis of the situation produces wobbly answers, dig deeper and make an objective decision.

The Go Quiz

Since there are so many moving parts to making the all important 'Go' decision, I developed a quick handy-dandy quiz that you and your senior team can take to help you to decide if you really want to spend the time and money to pitch this account. The quiz will even start to help you think through what you will need to say and do to win the business.

The quiz isolates a set of decision-making criteria and employs easy math to calculate your interest in actually pitching the account. You can, of course, add or subtract criteria. The point is to use some gray matter and time to make the right call. You do not have to pitch every account that comes knocking. In fact, don't.

Note: Since this is a strategic decision, and you really don't want to show your staff that you are taking a quiz to make the decision, I wouldn't put this quiz in front of the agency or the pitch team. It's just for management. OK, maybe you could share it after the fact to show that you are actually thinking through the Go decision-making process.

Each question has three answers ranked from 0 to 3. There is also a bonus question related to incumbency. If your total score is over 10 then you have no choice but to go for it. A 4 to 9 score is where you will have to use your gut and personal experience to make the decision. 3 or less and I'd think hard about ditching the pitch, and instead, take everyone in the agency out for a beer.

A note: All client, pitch, and agency motivations are different. You might want to modify this list depending on your own situation.

1. Do you know the decision maker?

0 – You've never talked to them.

1 – The client came to you through a personal referral.

2 – You are on a first name basis with the client. Maybe you've worked together in the past.

2. Do you have any history with the company?

0 – Never crossed paths.

1 – You worked with someone at the client who can vouch for the quality of your agency.

2 – You worked directly with the client or one of their brands in the past.

3. How professional is the client's agency selection process? Answer either the client or the agency search consultant questions only. (A or B, not both.)

A. Is the person running the pitch experienced?

0 – They have never ever run a pitch before.

1 – They are acting professionally.

2 – They have run pitches before and even sound like they are using the 4A's and ANA pitch guidelines.

B. Is the client is using a search consultant?

0 – You don't know the consultant.

1 – You have pitched the consultant in the past but lost.

2 – You have won business from the consultant.

4. Is the client in a category that your agency has targeted?

0 – No.

1 – Yes.

2 – Yes, and we have a dedicated business development effort to add clients in this specific category.

5. Do you have direct category experience?

0 – You have none. Um, what's a Widget?

1 – You have worked with a similar company or brand in the client's category.

2 – You are perceived as being a leading expert in the category. This is probably due to prior client experience and recognized thought-leadership.

6. Do you know the client's budget and / or how they plan to compensate the agency?

0 – You have no clue, and the client isn't forthcoming.

1 – The budget seems low, but you are willing to gamble.

2 – We're in the money!

7. Is the client looking for a "hot" award winning creative agency?

0 – You are creative but are not known for this.

1 – Recent campaigns have gotten you some industry attention.

2 – You have shelves full of Clios and were recently named to the ADWEEK Agency of the Year Something list.

8. Do you pitch well?

0 – Pitching hasn't been an agency strength.

1 – You have won a third of your pitches.

2 – You are so good at pitching that you have to pinch yourself.

9. How strong is your agency competition?

0 – They really kick ass, have a very high pitch batting average, and you should be worried.

1 – They are very similar to you.

2 – They look weak.

Ladies and gentlemen, your score is _____.

As a reminder: If your score is over 10 then you have no choice but to go for it. 4 to 9 is where you will have to use your gut to make the decision. Less than 3? It's Miller Time down at your local.

A Bonus Question: Are you the incumbent?

Just to complicate matters, are you the incumbent agency? If so, you need to think through why your beloved client has put the account up for grabs. Here is my simple litmus test.

1 – You have no clue why the client has put the account up for review.

Um, without knowing why, I'd back way off. It has been reported that only 10% of incumbents keep their account.

2 – You are the incumbent, and this is one of those pre-scheduled procurement-driven reviews. You know that the client loves you.

I'd go for it.

OK, Go.

If the client has passed your Go Quiz, then it's time to get to work.

I want to help and support you by working together to review all of the issues and opportunities that come with pitching and to help you use this book to win.

Managing how you craft your pitch, your time, and your staff will allow you to have the best possible pitch response ahead of your presentation deadline.

CHAPTER **3**

WHAT CLIENTS WANT

The Facts

If you have been asked to pitch a desirable account, everyone at your agency will soon know that you have been selected as a finalist. If you are going to move ahead, it's time to manage the information flow to your colleagues and their emotions.

Start with sharing the facts. Facts are good.

Once the agency has made the decision to move forward with the pitch, I suggest that you write a one-page document for the agency's 'need to know group' (and the pitch team if already selected) that includes key client information, the assignment, and your understanding of how and why you have been invited to pitch. Deliver the key facts and begin to anticipate your team's questions. This simple step will align the agency behind facts, not conjecture.

Some client pitch documents are well written and include all, if not most, of the basic corporate background information, marketing challenges, and pitch selection information. That said, it's safe to assume that the client or search consultant hasn't helped you build a competitive perspective for your agency. That's your job.

Your one-page document on the facts should begin to answer the following questions and begin to set up your pitch:

1. **Who is the client company?** In addition to studying the company website, check out Wikipedia, use company information sites like Access Confidential, Hoovers, and The List Online, and spend time going deep on Google to read press archives. Another great resource is the company website's investor relations section where you can read the client's detailed annual report and SEC 10-K filings. This can be very revealing. Your VC friends know all about 10-K's.

2. **What is this pitch for?** Is it for a corporate account, a brand, a specific service? A short or long relationship? Summarize what they are asking you to pitch for.

3. **What is the client's mission?** You can usually find the corporate Mission Statement on the client's website. I like to look at the Mission because many companies instill their mission into their workforce's psyche. You should know what and how the group thinks. You can build rapport if you know how they think and act.

   Sara Lee says, "*To simply delight you... every day.*" Hmm, I can begin to see the basis for a pitch platform and verbiage falling out of this clear statement.

4. **Who is the lead client executive and/or agency pitch consultant?** Start with the facts and a bio. We will come back to how to scope out the psychology of client decision makers a bit later. Knowing who is in the room will be critical to your success.

5. **Are you appropriately experienced?** List what, if any, experience the agency and your staff has with the client company, the client's people, its brands or category. It would be nice to have a simple pre-existing database of agency staff experience.

6. **What other agencies are in the pitch?** This is usually the second question agency staff asks after "who's the client?" Knowing who else is pitching delivers a range of information and will start to set up your response and presentation. Even though this is still early in the process, be prepared with the following discussion points as these will be extremely important to your staff. Your team will frame the pitch by knowing the competition and will start to guess at your chances of winning. The questions:

Who are the competitive agencies?

Is one the incumbent? Do you think that they are a lock to stay in place?

What are the pros and cons for each agency?

What is the personality and culture of the competitive agencies?

How do you think you stack up?

What Clients Want

After you have covered the basics with your team, it's time to start to begin to craft the presentation outline via a deep dive into this client's head.

From a pure sales perspective, this is the hottest type of lead your agency will ever get. This client is motivated and has been thinking about their needs for a while. They have put in the time to launch their process. They are very serious. They asked you to participate and want to like you.

Empathy please. Agency selection is hard work for clients. They know that poor decisions at the beginning of the pitch process will lead to selecting the wrong agency and will therefore cost time, money and possibly delay the market share gains they need. CMOs want to look like they are making the right decisions. New CMO's need to look sharp fast.

The Three Questions

In my experience, clients start their agency search process by asking three questions.

1. What is the specific assignment?

2. What type of type of relationship are we looking for?

3. What type of agency do we need?

1. Type Of Assignment

In a best-case scenario, the client has done their internal homework and has been transparent in telling you what they require from the scope, timing, and compensation structure of the assignment. You've determined this from a deep read of their pitch request document, and in the best-case scenario, you have had a chance to meet with the client and ask questions.

The savvy client has used a smart internal or search consultant-guided process to get to this stage.

They have (or should have):

- Committed to a deliberate process from needs assessment through an RFI and RFP agency process to get to the final short list.

- Defined their sales, market share, and ROI objectives.

- Agreed on scope of work.

- Set a budget and compensation scheme.

- Picked a search team and identified a decision-making system.

- Closely examined a range of possible agencies.

- Interviewed agencies to get to a finalist list.

2. Type Of Relationship

You should be able to determine what type of relationship the client is looking for – and why. Some relationships are unquestionably worth your effort. Some might not be.

The fall 2013 report "4A's and ANA Guidelines for Agency Search" outlines six types of agency relationships. I've listed them as described by the 4A's and ANA (Association of National Advertisers) in order of desirably and added my personal take on what this could mean for you:

Agency of Record (AOR) Search – An AOR relationship usually sets long-term strategic and communications direction for a brand (i.e., ongoing retainer-based relationships).

> My take: Although getting more rare, AOR assignments are the Holy Grail. An AOR relationship should deliver a higher pitch ROI due to long-term agency revenues. Take an all-in approach that demonstrates that you will be a dedicated agency partner that will invest in the client's success for the long haul.

Specialty Agency Search – These are agencies that have a specific expertise (e.g., mobile, event marketing, digital, social, media planning, or CRM). These agencies often supplement an AOR relationship or an existing roster.

> My take: Sweet. You have a skill that the client needs and cannot get from their current agencies. The client really needs what you have to offer. The bad news is that you might be up against similar specialist agencies. How you position your agency to create differentiation between the other specialists will be key.

Ad-hoc/Tactical Agency Searches – Typically smaller to mid-sized agencies used for more routine, turnkey work at a lower cost with a shorter turnaround time. These agencies can complement other agencies on the roster and free up core agencies to do more strategic work.

My take: Again, this is a good one. Small to mid-sized agencies know that getting that first foot in the door can lead to additional assignments and that all-important opportunity to excel and build a personal relationship. While the client is looking to fill a very specific need, you should be able to show that you have the skills and depth to be on their agency roster.

Project Reviews – Client searches for an agency to perform a specific, one-time deliverable.

My take: Projects can be a pain in the butt. They are short term, eat up staff time and can be inefficient from a pitch ROI perspective. But, like the tactical agency search, if it gets you in the door and if the client is large enough, go for it.

Roster Agency Search – Could involve a review for a specific assignment or might entail a qualified vendor status review with no specific assignment as part of the roster review. A roster agency is one that has met the criteria to be considered for a client's brands but may not yet have been awarded a brand assignment.

My take: Boy, this is a tough one. Is it worth the effort? Is it a fishing expedition run by a junior client or consultant looking to grow their agency information database? Tough to figure out if you should go for it or not. The ROI on this type of search is much lower – or will take a long time to pay off. You will have to decide if the long-term business opportunity outweighs the short-term pain.

International Agency Search – This is a search for an AOR to manage a global brand. This search is usually done to identify a lead office in a core market, which will then coordinate efforts with other offices around the world.

My take: These are usually multi-national network agency searches. However, I've worked with mid-sized agencies in Europe and Asia that have pitched across borders, so I think that there are more agencies pursuing international accounts than we think. If you are a medium size agency, note that big clients are well aware of the inefficiencies of working with massive agencies, and many have been seeking smaller specialist or creative-focused shops to work across their markets.

3. Type Of Agency

Once the client knows what kind of relationship they are seeking, they will think through the type of agency they need to meet their needs.

Here is my short list of agency types and how you might position your agency based on pitch-oriented typecasting:

Regional Leader – No one knows your local or regional market better than you. Your market-driven reputation drives your new business success. There are agencies that are asked to every regional or local pitch simply because they have been around forever, know their markets, and thrive on referrals.

Creative Hero – Your work stands out, gets discussed, has won awards, and builds market share in competitive categories. Clients want creative agencies (it is an essential part of what we offer), but creativity is in the eye of the beholder and can be difficult to demonstrate – especially when pitching less experienced clients.

Full Service Provider – Our industry has gone back and forth on the value of the full-service agency. I sense that we are currently experiencing a shift towards full service agencies that can deliver an integrated approach. There are so many moving parts to marketing today that some clients are becoming overwhelmed and need a single strategic partner that can help build an integrated plan. There is agency selection research that backs this up.

The Specialist – You have positioned your agency as an expert. You could be a mobile, social media, content, experiential, PR, or digital expert. The list of specialization opportunities keeps growing. Maybe you are a Vine or data visualization expert. If you are, and the client is looking for a Vine program, then you could be *exactly* what they need.

Strategic Guide and Resource – You have developed a reputation for your strategic insights and guidance. You've solved tough client problems in the past and have the cases to prove it.

Category Market Expert – You know the client's category better than any other agency. You've supported this fact with extensive client category history and a thought-leadership program.

Target Market Expert – No agency knows the client's target market and consumers better than you.

Big – When I ran business development at Saatchi & Saatchi, we led every pitch with a global map showing all of the Saatchi offices. I called it our dot map. We had dots everywhere. Big multinational clients want integrated global services and an agency that can run campaigns across borders. These clients need (or think they need) big networks and lots of dots. The downside of big is that clients can feel like they will get lost inside a huge agency, that not all of the agency dots are created equal, and that the agency's moving parts don't work synergistically.

Into The Client's Head

Now that you have a macro understanding of what assignment + relationship + type of agency selection criteria decisions the client has made, it's time to go deeper into developing a more fine-tuned assessment of what they *really* want.

Getting into the client's head can make or break your success rate.

As you move through your pitch development process, work to understand what this client is actually looking for and why they actively selected you.

Here is a place to start. You can always ask.

My agency Citrus did consumer advertising for Providence Health and Services, a huge 80,000-employee west coast health care organization. One day we were invited to pitch their employee recruitment account. Recruitment? Really?

We were not recruitment specialists but were asked to pitch against two very experienced experts: JWT Inside and Bernard Hodes. Before committing to the pitch, I asked "*Why us?*" The client's answer wooed me. I was told that we were included because we *weren't* a recruitment agency and might come in with new solutions. We did just that and won the business.

There are many scenarios for how you might have gotten invited into a pitch. For the sake of argument, we'll use what is a relatively standard path taken by experienced clients. Less sophisticated clients are harder to read since they probably didn't do a great job of providing a detailed pre-pitch brief.

In a best-case scenario, you received an RFI. You answered the basic information, met the client's initial criteria, and moved onto a more detailed RFP.

You answered the questions, provided requested information, may have started to dazzle them with some strategic insights, and are starting to think that you know what this client is looking for. Maybe you do and maybe not.

If you are brilliant or just lucky, you've made it to the finalist stage. You have to be thinking that this client digs your stuff. Regardless, you are now in deep and have to compete with other finalist agencies for the account. Obviously, the client must dig the other agency's stuff too.

Since each agency search is unique, there will be particular requirements for individual clients. That said, based on client agency selection research and my experience, the great majority of clients are looking for one or all of these four attributes from their new agency.

The Four Sweet Spots

1. **Strategic thinking and guidance.** The client is looking for an agency that is skilled at converting a business objective into a strategic communications program that delivers measurable results.

2. **Creativity.** This is the agency's ability to convert a strategy into a compelling communications program that gets the attention of the target market and turns them into a "liker" or better, a buyer.

3. **Category or target market expertise, or both.** Prior experience is like comfort food for clients.

4. **And then there is all-important chemistry.** Chances are good that you will be up against look-alike agencies. You all probably share similar attributes, skills, and histories. You might even be wearing the same Armani suit or Tory Burch shoes.

Because of this, the ultimate selection factor is often based on personal vibes. The client wants to feel comfortable with and inspired by the agency's culture and people. They are looking for a dedicated partner who will care as much about their business as they do. They want a *confident* agency that looks, acts, and feels right.

I can't stress the chemistry thing enough. Here is what Avidan Strategies' 2012 survey of agency search consultants revealed:

> *"Practically every consultant, or 96% of the sample, pointed to "chemistry" as the key factor for winning. But what exactly is chemistry? Generally speaking it is simpatico between the client and agency teams."*

So while you are thinking about how to express your agency's core skills and style, remember that how you express who you are could be the make or break part of your pitch. I'll talk more about chemistry later. But it is imperative that you keep personal chemistry in mind as you start to think through what this client *really* wants.

Oh, The Competition

There is another angle into the client's head and that is through your review of the other finalist agencies. This list should be very revealing on many fronts.

Before I get into the value of knowing the finalist agency list, we need to address the fact that in some cases we don't actually know who the competition is. I asked the CEO of an international agency recently if they knew what agencies they are pitching against. His answer, "Never. Well, rarely." Never. Rarely. Huh. Now, why wouldn't the client divulge the list? This CEO said that clients don't want the word getting out because they fear being inundated with calls from other agencies, and they believe that their short list is proprietary.

I file this thinking into my "lame file".

Yo, clients. You are about to ask a bunch of agencies to spend thousands of dollars to pitch for your business, and you don't want to share your agency list? Get over it. Really. If NASA can tell competing rocket companies who is on their short list, you can list the ad agencies you've asked to pitch for your business.

The good (smart) client divulges which agencies are in the pitch. The list of participating agencies will help your agency understand what the client is looking for and will assist you in building a better case for your agency that, in the end, will help the client have more information to make their selection. That's the best case. A worse case is when you realize that the client does not look like it has done its agency selection homework or a very good job of building a logical short list. I've heard of pitches where big Ogilvy is pitching against small specialist agencies. Too many disparate agencies on the short list is a bad sign that the client has no clue what skills and type of service it wants from an agency. If the client's list is a total head scratcher, consider backing away, or at least use the list as a good reason to ask for more information.

The competitor list will help you begin to understand how you will need to create a distinctive story and how to frame your agency's credentials, expertise, related history, and insights. You will also begin to understand how to build your pitch team to outshine the other agency's core culture and personality.

Knowing the competition and where you fit in might deliver a valuable 'However Moment'. The list might convince you that you are an extreme long shot and that you have been asked to the party just to round out the short list. Outlier agencies do win pitches (remember, my agency won that healthcare recruitment account). However, you should really think through your odds. If they are too steep, maybe this is a pitch you should pass up.

Here is a way to manage the competitive decision.

Build a quick competitive matrix or SWOT analysis to find where you can shine and where the other agencies might fail. If you are up against Droga5 you might just win because you are a small mobile specialist, have your very own Brooklyn-born hipster ECD that can out Droga-speak Droga5, and are just down the street from a client that really craves frequent human contact.

CHAPTER **4**

TEACHABLE MOMENTS

The 12 Deadliest Presentation Mistakes

We have all been at the receiving end of sales calls where the sales person makes a critical gaff that destroys his chances of making the sale. You know the exact moment when it happens. He might know it as well. The only way to *not* make a critical mistake is to be very conscious of what your mistakes might be ahead of the sales call – study them, trash them, and practice for success.

The following set of mistakes is not in any particular order. You probably haven't made all of them. But I bet that you've made some. I know I have.

Understatement alert: Going back to a point that I am making over and over… by the very nature of the agency selection process indicates that there is a very good chance that your agency is similar to the other agencies that made it onto the short list. What isn't similar are *your* ideas and *your* personality. Making sure that your ideas get heard, that you deliver your most salient points with clarity and passion, *and* that you get to that very special agency-client eHarmony moment, can make or break your chances.

Here are my 12 *favorite* mistakes. Delivered as must do's.

I've purposely served the mistakes up as advice, as things *to* do. Why? Because as you will see throughout this book (especially in the interview section) many agencies, pitch leaders, and team members make these crazy mistakes. According to agency search consultants, these mistakes are made all the time. Agencies make them despite knowing that they will lower the their batting average. This is quite baffling.

To help resolve this dilemma, I offer my 12 deadliest mistakes as counter-intuitive must dos illustrated by series of cartoons from my friend Steve Klinetobe and his company The Cartoon Agency.

Immediately bore them.

There are many paths to achieving immediate boredom. Personally, I like fumbling with the freakin' projector and connector thing, not making eye contact, forgetting your manners, and of course, bringing on some very obvious flop sweat.

Well, watching *you* flop sweat might actually be interesting to them.

Don't be distinctive.

In fact, be very afraid of looking too different.

Why take the chance of building agency brand differentiation when your unique flavor might make you look and sound *too* different from the other agencies?

Don't have a logical flow.

Deliver your presentation without a clear start, middle and end. Don't build to any decisive Wow! Moments or give your audience enough time to absorb what you are saying.

Oh, and don't leverage the power of presenting problems and solutions that are directly related to the client's pain points.

STEP 4
LOAD THE ROOM WITH AGENCY STAFF

Load up the room with agency staff.

Make sure that you arrive with a large posse. In fact, have so many people that by the end of the meeting the client won't even be able to remember any single individual, what they do at the agency, or what they said.

Use your numbers to crowd the room and destroy any opportunity to build person-to-person chemistry. Make your presentation like dating quintuplets.

Way out-number the clients so they begin to worry about how you will pad your billable hours.

Bring on your poorest presenters.

In this case, bring the inarticulate art director, the untrained media super star, and the way-junior AAE just because she worked on the pitch every night for two months. It's a great reward for her.

You are a great people manager.

STEP 6

DON'T FORGET TO "ME-ME"

Don't Forget To "Me-Me."

The client invited you to pitch. That means that they want to hear every possible fact about your agency, people, history, and past client stories. Make sure that you repeat every bit of information previously delivered in your RFI and RFP response.

And make sure that you don't spend your valuable time talking about the client's issues or opportunities. Act like you didn't even bother to read their briefing documents.

Use your precious time to go "Me-Me."

Present tons of strategic ideas.

It's a numbers game, and you better ensure that you dilute your best ideas with a range of mediocre ideas because, well, the client might not agree with what *you* think is "best."

Presenting lots of ideas is easier than trying to sell one great one. Because your great idea might not be *their* great one and having an agency point-of-view is so overrated.

Show them lots of creative work.

Remember, it's a numbers game. Yeah, it's déjà vu time again.

Since you have no way of knowing what solutions would be of interest to them, show a massive amount of creative work. Prove how productive you are.

Beat it into them.

Don't rehearse.

Make sure that everyone on your team arrives being unsure of their role, how all of the pieces flow together, and how sections will be handed off from one presenter to another.

Or better yet, have the CEO or ECD come in the night before the pitch to rearrange the presentation by adding their last-minute touch of brilliance.

STEP 10
MISUSE POWERPOINT

Misuse PowerPoint.

Ignore everything you have ever heard about how to effectively use PowerPoint or any other presentation tool. Make sure that your screen is the star of your show – not you, that you have loads of copy on each slide, keep your fonts tiny, use lots of bullet points, and remember to face the screen more than your audience.

Reduce direct eye contact whenever possible.

Don't stage-manage.

Show up without knowing how long the meeting is scheduled for, how many clients will be in the room, who they are, who the decision maker is, and have no clue about the layout of the presentation room or available technologies.

Remember, spend the first ten minutes of your allotted sixty screwing around with the computer to projector connection.

Be prepared to just wing it. You've always wanted to do improv.

STEP 12

RUN OUT OF TIME

Run out of time.

I love this one. There is nothing that beats that sweet feeling you will get when the client starts to stand up and leave the room before you had a chance to finish your presentation.

To get to this wonderful moment, remember to not time your presentation, or plan for discussion and questions, or instruct your presenters to reduce their adlibbing.

12 big ones. Yowser.

Yeah, I know I am being Mr. Negative. If I thought that my list of big time mistakes didn't bear mentioning… I wouldn't have.

However, if my perspective makes an impression that begins to force you to think through and manage every potential failure point of your presentation, then you just got supremo value from this book.

CHAPTER **5**

THE LEVITAN PITCH SYSTEM

Now you know what *not* to do (ever, please). What follows is what you have to do to increase your batting average.

At this point, your agency has been asked to the dance, they've been alerted about the facts of the pitch, and you have started to think about what it might take to win. Your job is to manage what is often a very unwieldy process. After all, today's agencies are already working at a high staff utilization rate.

Here are 6 cornerstone steps that will help you to begin building the foundation of winning pitch. I will elaborate further on all of these points. For now, they are the starting point.

1. **Select the master team.** Depending on your agency structure and your role in the pitch, you will need to select two groups to work on the pitch. The first group includes the people who will do the actual face-to-face presentation, and the second includes supporting cast of strategists, creatives, and production managers who will craft the pitch but will not be going to the presentation.

2. **Select the presenters.** Some presenters might be a given, like the agency CEO or the effervescent Steve Jobs-like Creative Director. However, there is no one size-fits-all team, and you will need to study what the client is looking for and their collective personas before you make this critical decision.

    You should start with your agency's best presenters – actually best *persuaders* – and how many will be needed for this particular pitch. Remember the Adidas story. This isn't about egos, seniority, or "it's my turn" to pitch. This is all about the perfect fit of your presentation team based on their presentation skills, intelligence, expertise, and the type of client that you are going to persuade to hire you.

    Of course, this decision can become complicated because some clients are very specific about who they want to meet, like their day-to-day contacts, and these people might not be your best presenters. If so, give them a role but keep their section shorter than that of your "A-Team" presenters. If they are not experienced presenters, find a way to enhance their presentation skills *before* you walk into the presentation. Consider force-feeding them a small diet of killer TED presentations. I'll have more on this important subject later.

3. **Create a pitch timetable.** Work backwards from the actual pitch to adequately schedule pitch planning, research, writing, creative development, production, travel, and any other tasks. This schedule will surely be modified as you move through pitch development. However, you need to begin to plot out your workload, and you want the pitch team to see that there is a plan. Poor planning leads to an overburdened and burnt-out crew that can't deliver their best work. Last minute all-nighters can be a losing proposition.

4. **Establish a working budget.** Pitches are expensive. Starting out with a budget for internal agency costs and out of pocket expenses will help control your budget. If this sounds obvious, it isn't for most pitches. In fact, ask if your agency even has an annual business development budget.

You don't want to run out of biz dev cash weeks before your December 12th pitch.

5. **Perform a pitch SWOT.** Use a SWOT analysis to determine your agency's strength's, weaknesses, opportunities, and threats related to this pitch, including the competition. It will help you objectively determine what agency attributes to highlight and which weaknesses need some tender care. Think like the client.

6. **Write a pitch Creative Brief.** You wouldn't start a client job without one. For the same strategic reasons, do it for yourself.

Oh, there is one more critical step. Make sure that everyone involved with the pitch understands that there are 12 key mistakes that are made over and over again by even the best agencies and presenters. Yes, just like my baby seals, making even one of these mistakes could kill any chance you have of winning your pitch. The key to success is knowing what the deadliest mistakes are and making a commitment to not make them.

Tip:

Pin up the 12 Deadliest Presentation Mistakes cartoons.

Part One: Process

I know that you know that I know that you know what I am about to tell you.

However, I also know that *despite* your knowing, you need to be reminded that if you don't concentrate on managing the pitch and the presentation development process itself – you will reduce the odds of winning your pitch.

How did we get to a place where we all, and I am talking about small, medium and large agencies, can still make *déjà vu all over again* mistakes about pitching and delivering brilliant presentations? We are all communications experts; many of us have pitched our agency stories to prospective clients for years, we've worked to learn from past winners and mistakes, we've read shelves of expert books on presenting (the best are listed on my website), and we've watched TED conference speakers kill it.

Somehow, in the excitement and heat of pitch preparation, the one thing that gets shunted to the side is stopping to think hard about how we are going to manage the process.

OY, process.

Look, I realize that we all approach pitching differently. This is the result of past experiences and personal orientation. Some of us are "left-brained" and are more logical and objective. Our "right-brained" colleagues are generally more intuitive, thoughtful and subjective. So, while there may never be that one size fits all approach, we still need some guidelines and should have an established process that uses all of the agency's resources to best advantage. Oh, and to prevent making any silly mistakes. Again.

The Chosen One

Every pitch needs its Chosen One – the pitch leader. This leader will be the guide and decision maker and will be fully supported by agency management. I see a pitch leader having five critical attributes:

1. **The brains to get it right.** Everyone at the agency must believe that the Chosen One has the skills and experience to run a winning pitch, understands the client's needs, and how to marshal and use the agency's talent and use it efficiently.

2. **Leadership and respect.** The team and agency management must respect the leader's ability to lead the team and to manage the process.

3. **Personal responsibility.** The leader must take and use his responsibility. He is where the buck stops.

4. **Attention to detail.** Pitches are comprised of tiny details. Failure at any single point can kill the pitch and presentation. The leader will

have the brains and detail orientation to keep everything on track. Attention deficit disorder does not work in the land of pitching. A bit of obsessive-compulsive disorder just might.

5. **Time.** The leader has to have the time to plan and manage pitch development. Brains, leadership, and respect are worthless unless he/she has the time to devote to this effort. Starting pitch meetings at 6PM because the leader is sooo busy with existing clients will reduce the agency's odds of winning and will quickly erode pitch team passion.

Tip:

Create an internal decision matrix for selecting each pitch's Chosen One. If you are a small agency, the CEO might be the default leader. Larger agencies should consider a set of attributes including seniority, pitch management experience, personal presentation skills, R-E-S-P-E-C-T (because they will be asking busy agency folks to work even harder), and client category history.

Selecting the Chosen One because they are the only one with free time is a big mistake.

Deconstruction

The first thing the Chosen One needs to do, and take the time to get right, is to stop and read, and then carefully deconstruct the client's brief.

Now, why do I think that I need to state this rather obvious point? Because over the years, clients and search consultants have repeatedly told me that many agencies do not address all of the questions and issues that clients raise in pitch documents. It starts with poor RFP responses that miss the details and ends with agencies not covering the points that the client needs addressed in the final presentation. Head scratcher, right?

Some clients are very clear about what they want. Other briefs will require you to read between the lines. Just make sure that you give yourself the time to dig into the prose and to go Sigmund Freud if you have to. Your goal is to answer the questions, hit the obvious and not so obvious hot buttons, and to figure out how and where you are going to roll out your own pearls of wisdom.

Tip:

Have more than one senior person read the brief. If it is long, parse out sections and have experienced people dig into one section at a time. Use your left-brain attention-to-detail team members. Consider role-playing where you ask one team member to hone in on what they think the client *wants* to hear and another to hone in on what they think the agency *needs* to hear to win the account. See if they match. This is your chance to find an angle that will be different from what all the other agencies might be focusing on.

Zero in

In my experience, there is usually one seminal moment in a presentation when the client makes up their mind. This can be a rational, irrational, or even emotional decision (like they've decided that they really like your sense of humor or your tattoo). Regardless of the reason, there is usually some point when they come to the realization that you are the best agency to help them achieve their objectives.

You might not be able to read the client's mind, or get a preview of their selection scorecard. But you are a communications professional and should be able to make a very educated guess ahead of the meeting about the one or two things you need to do or say that will get you to a win. Base your guess on your hard read of the brief, your examination of their market, and your conversations with the client.

Tip:

I can't imagine developing a pitch without a clear sense of what you think you need to accomplish to win. Write that pitch creative brief, with a section on client personas, very early in the process. How could you plan your presentation with out this strategic document? To help, I have a sample presentation creative brief in my online Playbook.

Another approach is to isolate and fit your primary must-have messages – the one or two things you need to say to win – on index cards, and keep them front and center while your team writes the pitch. This will force the team to focus and hone their primary messages. And, reinforce these in each section.

The Checklist

Leading a pitch isn't easy. The pitch leader is juggling their current client workload, the client's documents, communications with the client or search consultant, the timetable, agency staff, pitch-related research, presentation materials, travel plans, meeting room logistics, technology decisions, and so on.

Forgetting one simple thing, like the cable thingy that connects a laptop to the projector, will make you all look unorganized in front of the client. You know what I am talking about.

Tip:

Create an agency presentation development checklist right now. Everything you do will flow from that. Don't forget any elements. Assign responsibilities to all items. Use my playbook checklist as a start. It will help your most attention-deprived colleagues focus on their specific tasks. You don't want to be on the road to the presentation with distracting questions like, "Umm, who has the leave behind?" A sample checklist is in the Playbook.

The Budget

Establish a budget for the pitch. Base it on the perceived value of the account. Spending $25,000 to win a one-off project assignment that will (hopefully) deliver $30,000 in profit 120 days after the pitch isn't good business. If the client is Kraft, Toyota, or Uber, it might be worth a gamble. But it's not a smart roll of the dice if it's Widgets, Inc.

Tip:

Use the pitch checklist, and price out all of the elements that you think you will need to build a winning pitch. Try to use this to control your costs. I say try because I am a realist, and things do happen. That said, this is one element of the pitch that you do have virtually 100% control over. Take it.

Take The Time

If you don't give yourself the time to get it right, you probably won't get it right.

Pitches are by nature sprints. Depending on the pitch, you might need to do research, dig into your agency's history to find relevant cases, build insights, write strategies, write copy, create art, make videos, think through media and social media options, and study the competition. If you don't manage the time to complete this complex process, you might not get it right. Or worse, you get it right a couple of days after the presentation.

Managing your time should be easy. Build a pitch development calendar with team responsibilities. Work it backwards from the minute you deliver your leave behind. Presentation development is like a funnel that includes analysis of the client's brief, strategic and creative development, present-er selection, scripting, production, etc. Each stage must be given time to blossom. The funnel will be wide at the beginning and gets real tight by the day before you pitch. Plan for this.

Consider that your Managing Director or ECD could be your worst time-crunch offender. If they need to see the presentation before you finalize it, pick a date for them to have their say. If you really want to win the sprint, get them involved early. I have seen presentations ruined by having to shoehorn in 'brilliant' senior manager insights at the last minute.

Tip:

Before you start to write your presentation, use my pitch checklist to think through all the elements and must-have's of the pitch, and how much time they might take to complete.

Why not create a standard pitch timetable for your agency? Most pitches share similar objectives and tasks, and you won't always have to start from scratch.

Tame The Meeting

Speaking of time, poorly managed agency meetings waste time, kill creativity, and cost money. They could also help you lose your pitch.

As pitch team leader, your job is to manage the pitch process so that the agency will deliver the best response it can. I've always believed that meeting management is one of the first places to start. It should be ingrained into agency culture.

In 1986, I moved from New York to reopen Dancer Fitzgerald Sample's Minneapolis office and manage the Northwest Airlines account. I was invited into the client's inner circle and attended their senior management meetings as the advertising agency representative. These were the good old days when an experienced agency's opinion on marketing and even in-flight service was considered critical to C-Suite success.

I quickly realized that the airline had a serious meeting problem. Most of my clients were in non-stop meetings from 8AM to 6PM. I couldn't figure out when they had time to think, let alone get their jobs done. This fact wasn't lost on the airline's COO who hired a management consultant to help create an efficient and effective meeting culture. It was instructive to watch this course correction help Northwest make faster decisions and become the fastest growing airline in the late 1980's.

Effective meetings deliver three key benefits:

1. Effective meetings focus on and achieve meeting objectives.

2. Well-managed meetings take up a minimum amount of time.

3. Participants leave the meeting feeling that a sensible process has been followed and that their time has been used effectively.

I've incorporated the meeting consultant's advice into my agency culture since the 90's. I suggest that you incorporate these meeting management rules at your agency and consider posting them in the conferences rooms. These rules are especially important in the fast-paced agency pitch scenario. They work and will help alleviate some of the problems that agency staff has with the pitch process. You will also look like you are on the ball.

Meeting Rules:

1. Every meeting must have a leader to create and manage an agenda.

2. Invite only the people that need to be in the meeting. This isn't a numbers game.

3. Time management is critical. Make sure that anyone needed in the meeting knows of the start and stop time. There shouldn't be any open-ended meetings. This is critical.

4. Everyone must understand that they are required to show up on time, and if they are late, they will be costing the agency time and money. Keeping colleagues waiting is rude and costly. Do the math on the time staff sits around waiting for a colleague to eventually show up.

5. State the meeting objectives at the start of the meeting.

6. Once an objective is met, move on to the next one. Stay on topic.

7. Watch the clock, and end the meeting when you have covered the objectives. Consider using a meeting timer. Google does.

8. State any follow-up items, timing, and individual responsibilities. Send out a meeting summary.

Believe me, well-run meetings are refreshing.

Tip:

These rules, in a modified fashion (don't be too controlling), should be considered in how you mange the client presentation. Clients will respect you when you show respect for their time and show that your agency is well managed. I'll cover how to mange the presentation in the presentation section.

The War Room

The "War Room." I'd love to come up with a better name for pitch central, but I won't even try. War room works because it frames the pitch process as being a life or death event. And for many agencies, it just might be.

Pitch war rooms come in different sizes and shapes, but the best agencies use a conference room or office that is dedicated to the pitch. The war room serves multiple objectives.

1. It is the hub for the pitch and focuses the pitch team on the task at hand.

2. It provides a physical format for framing the issues.

3. It includes a large timetable used to track responsibilities based on the client's pitch document and assigned tasks.

4. It is the pitch library where all members of the pitch team can go to find relevant information and materials including the pitch request document, samples of the client's product or service, research, the client's annual report, PR, news articles, etc.

5. War room walls aid visual stimulation by showing existing marketing work for the client and their competition. Consider pinning up visual personas of the client's target audiences. While you are at it, pin up photos and bios of the clients that will be in the pitch. Put names to faces and get to know them.

Tip:

If your team travels for a living, consider building a mobile online war room where you can store all of your digital information, timetables, assignments, and valuable links so that the war room goes from static to interactive and portable. Use your agency intranet or digital management and collaboration tools like Basecamp, ProofHub and Siasto. If you are a very mobile or virtual agency, I suggest that you start to plan how to build a mobile war room today.

Part Two: Content

Client Think

I ran client companies twice in my career. I had to select agencies to bring my two well-funded Internet startups to life via advertising and public relations. Being a client after 16 years in the agency business and running new business made the agency selection a fascinating experience. My decision-making was predicated on rational *and* emotional factors.

My Rational Needs:

1. I needed very smart partners.

2. I needed to know that the agency was strategic and that they had a track record of converting brand strategy into compelling creative solutions.

3. I needed to know that the agency had the skills and knowledge of my industry and consumers required to do the job.

4. I wanted to see case histories that had relevance to my business objectives.

5. I needed to know that the agency believed in my service, took the time to understand the competitive environment, and that they were passionate about the opportunity to help my company grow.

6. I paid close attention to what they chose to present, and how their ideas and vision were going to benefit me and meet my objectives. This was an opportunity for me to judge their decision-making and communication skills.

7. I needed to know that they were good at sales. If they couldn't sell themselves, they couldn't sell my service.

Emotional Needs:

1. I wanted to work with people I liked. It took about ten minutes to figure out if I wanted to spend long hours with these people.

2. I needed them to demonstrate passion and chutzpah. I wanted to work with high-energy people. I was in startup mode. Plodding wouldn't work in that space.

3. I wanted to know that they were good listeners.

4. I like people that take chances and are opinionated.

5. Having a sense of humor was a major plus.

Tip:

Use the presentation Creative Brief to force your team to think like your audience. You have their pitch document, you have determined the client's major needs, you know their history, you did some intelligence gathering, and you studied their corporate culture and individual personalities. Use this information to think like the client. You do this for your existing clients. Just do the same thing for yourself.

Building insights.

I admit it. I am a closet account planner. I love the art of unearthing consumer insights and building strategies. My first New York agency trained its AE's to be strategic client guides, had a 15-person research group, a long list of proprietary research tools, and a large multi-stack research library with a dedicated librarian that we used for client and new business research. We had researchers, psychologists, and even anthropologists to do field work. Back in the 1980's using anthropology to help create advertising was so rare that we branded our anthropological study the Anthropological Probe (yes, we recognized the humor in the name).

Our consumer insights delivered outstanding advertising like "You asked for it, you got it. Toyota." and "Where's the beef?" Our approach resulted in an industry-leading new business batting average of .900.

When I moved to London, I was blown away by the intelligence and creative power of Saatchi's world of account planning. While we had all those smart, somewhat academic 'research' folks in New York, London had all-black clad account planning super stars. As the decade progressed, American agencies eventually imported some of these English-accented thinkers to help us get and sound smarter to help us retain and add new clients.

Today, due to the ad industry's belt tightening, there are fewer planners. At the same time, clients say that strategic chops are one of the top three things they look for in an agency. That said, the gap between clients wanting but not willing to pay for insights is perplexing.

Our need for consumer insights has been amplified by our search for intelligent pathways through the growing density of media options and data overload. Fortunately, while all of us can't afford a BBDO-sized account-planning group, we now have a long list of low cost to free Internet-based tools at our disposal. Many of these tools provide real-time information and help us parse big-data. Today, all agencies should be able to build insights without the need for actual planners. If you are Internet savvy, you can look and sound like an account planner. Well, you might not be able to fake the English accent.

I've won pitches with business-building insights, and I'd imagine that you have too. In fact, I've recognized and loved the moment when our team hit a strategic homerun. You can see it in the client's eyes.

What insights can you deliver? Let's take this question a bit further and add in one of today's beloved marketing terms:

Big Data.

To rephrase… What big data inspired insights can you deliver?

Every CMO, marketing, and sales department will have their own business goals, pain points, and information requirements. Tailor your insights to match the client's issues and opportunities. Importantly, make sure that you are not simply parroting what the client's industry discusses every day. *Your* insights better be insightful and unique. What do I mean by "insights"?

Insights are our capacity to discern the true nature of a situation.

They are the act or outcome of grasping the inward or hidden nature of things or of perceiving in an intuitive manner.

They are a penetrating and often sudden understanding of a complex situation or problem.

They are the platform for brilliant creative.

They deliver that all-important pitch winning Wow! Moment.

Here are seven direct data-to-insight thought starters that can be customized by client and category.

1. Compare competitor website stats including demographics, page views, unique visitors, seasonality, top keywords, etc.

2. Isolate competitive search (i.e. interest) trends, seasonality, geography, search ranking, keywords, device usage, and demographics.

3. Find geographic market opportunities.

4. Track real-time brand sentiment on Twitter and across blogs.

5. Make a category-related case for mobile or social or native or radio or experiential advertising.

6. Compare and contrast competitive brand positioning, mission statements, and advertising approaches to find competitive messaging opportunities.

7. Deep read brand Facebook pages and Twitter feeds. This might not sound like fun, but it's very revealing since you are essentially eavesdropping on honest real-time consumer conversations.

I suggest that you create and manage a big data insights tool kit. Most of these tools are free. A couple have nominal costs.

Note: Analytics is a big business. New big data insight tools are being launched every month. I stay tuned into this world by asking Google itself what's new by including dates. Want to be a social media expert? Try searching on "Twitter tools 2014." Another angle is to look for planner presentations on SlideShare and LinkedIn. You'll be surprised at how much valuable strategic information is being shared.

Today's list:

Plain Old Search. There isn't much I can add to what you know about search. However, there is one trick that might help save time to get you to the most professional data and information faster. I add "PDF" to my search phrases to help me find higher value documents.

Google Search Trends. Google Trends tracks search interest in specific topics over time. You can search on multiple terms to makes comparisons. I love this tool and use it all the time to make points with my agency clients via irrefutable graphics. I had an agency client that was wavering on the decision on whether or not they should add more UX services to their expertise mix. Google Trends showed that interest in the term "user experience" was experiencing a major growth spurt.

Google Keyword Tool. This tool is the Search Engine Optimization expert's Holy Grail. The Google Keyword Tool helps us research the specific search terms and phrases web users use. It delivers relative interest in competitors, their sales propositions, and device usage and shows what other, possibly unexpected, terms searchers are searching for related to the brand.

Facebook Analytics. Go to a Facebook page, click on Fans and Ta Da… Facebook gives you most popular city, weeks and age groups. It's not super detailed, but it can provide good data for comparing competitive social media activity.

Compete (and Quantcast). Compete tracks a range of Website visitor trends including traffic, keywords, and seasonality, and you can compare multiple sites. It's like having Google Analytics for the rest of the world. Compete and its competitor Quantcast can deliver much more detailed information including demographics, but these tools can get expensive. Try Compete for free for a day.

Twitonomy. Need a deep read into a brand's Twitter world? Twitonomy helps you to get detailed and visual analytics on anyone's tweets, retweets, replies, mentions, and hash tags.

Topsy. Topsy is a very cool Twitter analytics tool. It will show you what people are saying about a brand, number of tweets, sentiment score, category influencers, and more.

Consumer Barometer. Consumer Barometer uses Google search data to help understand how consumers use search in their purchase process.

eMarketer. I keep a file of marketing graphs from eMarketer. The good news is that eMarketer sends me these in daily emails. I've used these graphs on my website to prove points like the fact that your ad agency better start to really understand the essence of mobile marketing.

Creative Search. I occasionally need to find examples of advertising or digital campaigns to make a point. Two of my favorites tools are: the Digital Buzz blog, which helps me to search across digital campaign types like games, mobile marketing, and mobile programs and Ads Of The World which filters advertising by media, region, country, and industry.

Online surveys. Surveys will help you to confirm and sell-in your opinions and insights. There are over 25 online survey tools. You should be able to write, design, and field an online survey in less than 24 hours. Things to look for in evaluating survey tools include ease of survey building, survey logic (i.e. skip patterns), email distribution, responding scenarios, and analysis.

Secret or mystery shopper. This is one of the old standbys and for good reason. Agencies already use the secret shopper experience to help their clients understand a brand, product, or service from the consumer's perspective. Secret shopper studies include going on location, studying websites, and experiencing call centers. You can do this on your own or employ the service of vendors like IntelliShop.

Man on the street interviews. One more agency standby is the man on the street interview. I love them and have conducted them myself. All you need is a set of questions, a microphone, and a video camera. You could even use your smart phone. You might not be the only agency using this tactic, so think hard about making your mini-videos special.

JSS. Just Sounding Smart. If I am seeking information on industry trends, demographics, and the brightest minds on marketing, I use the Pew Internet and The Harvard Business Review. A few quotes and voila, I can sound brilliant on almost any subject.

Blogs. If I need a stimulating jolt from other people's thinking, I visit experts that live and breathe in the blogosphere. Virtually every product and service category has its own group of expert blogs.

I know that you know this, but just to prove my point, if you want to win the next California Milk Advisory Board pitch, go search on "dairy blogs" and you'll arrive at Proud To Dairy's list of dozens of dairy blogs.

For insights related to our industry, I head over to Ad Age's Power 150 list of advertising, digital and social media blogs and websites. Ad Age's #6 is Seth Godin's popular *Seth's Blog* – always a good source for idea generation. Note: Ad Age does not update this list any more. But, it is still up and provides a good starting list of advertising industry related blogs and their own blog lists.

Hire a research expert. If you are a savvy agency that gets into lots of pitches, you should have a very short list of research companies and account planners that you can turn to for expert help. In my experience, clients like expert researchers.

Tip:

To keep up with what's new do a once a month search on "social media tools", or "Twitter tools" or "mobile tracking tools" or whatever you want web-based tools for. There is a growing industry of tool suppliers and many of them offer their tools for free.

Case Histories

"Why is the agency taking the time to tell me this client story?"

"What does this case history have to do with my business objectives?"

Can you imagine using your case histories to force a client to ask themselves these questions in the middle of your pitch? It happens. Too often. It happens because agencies have their own beloved winners and agency-based cultural icons, and they want to make damn sure that the client hears about these in the pitch.

Look, I get it. Let's say that you were the agency that authored Oreos' timely 2013 Super Bowl Tweet… "You can still dunk in the dark." It was a winner: it was retweeted a bizillion times, it ushered in the idea of real-time marketing, and it won two Cannes Lions! Come on, you just have to include this case in your pitch right? Although this is a great story, I am going to suggest that you don't include it (or your own best loved but irrelevant story).

Why? I bet that you love it so much that you already used it in your earlier RFP response, and you are including it in your leave behind. Deep down, you also know that this truly wonderful marketing event does not really relate at all to the needs of Widget, Inc. Furthermore, you know that this CMO is a analytics freak, and she could be sitting there wondering if this famous Tweet actually moved any packages. Did it? Do you know? Which leads me to my next point.

We know from agency selection research that clients want to know that your agency understands the importance of measurable results and ROI. It's so 21st century.

Cases are the perfect presentation tool to prove that you dig results. I believe that to craft a winning case, it must include positive (as in real) results. These results should be expressed in client-speak: cost-per-sale, conversions, same store sales, YOY growth, 'measurable', and revenues. Why is this important? Cases work when they are used to give the client permission to believe that your agency relates to their objectives and business needs and that your creative solutions are strategically designed to move product or services. Today's CMO is rather bottom-line oriented. Their COO, CPO and CFO certainly are and this is how they judge the CMO's performance. So remember that other three-letter shorthand: ROI.

To better understand the business of how an agency might win a account by having a business-first orientation, I asked the very results-oriented automotive CMO Ian Beavis for his opinion on what is important to clients. This question first appeared in my *Advertising Week* article, "Dreaming Of A Car Account?" Ian is currently EVP Global Automotive Group at The Nielsen Company and was VP Marketing, Public Relations & Product Planning Kia Motors and SVP Mitsubishi Motors USA.

> **PL: Agencies have a hard time creating a competitive agency positioning. Any insights and advice you can give the agency world on how to be distinctive in this highly competitive category?**
>
> Ian: You rarely hear of an agency being a business solution provider, as it just doesn't sound cool or creative. A good agency solves a client's business issues and is a partner. Very few qualify and even fewer truly embrace this challenge.

OK, you got it right? Most agencies don't sound like business partners. Should I stop beating this business solutions provider message to death? Sorry I won't, because you have to use this message in your pitch.

Tip:

Use your cases to sound different from the other agencies by thinking about how you frame and express these case histories. Think about your terminology and that it might sound like every other agency. Sure, you can use the obvious and usual cast of characters: problems, issues, objectives, challenges, implementation, solutions, outcomes, and results terminology. Or you could go one big strategic step further and work at sounding different from every other agency pitching that day. LONDON Advertising has gone one big case study step beyond by branding their case study system.

They call their client strategic philosophy and cases, "Straight-Line Thinking". See how they deliver short but sweet cases on their website.

Spec Creative

I have been wrestling with the question of whether or not my agencies should do spec creative for new business pitches since my first pitch. I have never been able to answer that question with a definitive yes or no. I have never found a one-size-fits-all answer for all agencies and situations.

Why? Some of the factors that confuse the spec issue are legal, and some are emotional. Some come from a deep belief that a smart client should be able to look at your industry-leading creative work, client successes and dozens of awards to figure out that you are damn good at your job and don't need to do spec to prove it all over again. And as you will see later in the book, some clients just want to watch your creative process in action. This is one reason I can't argue with.

More thoughts on this tough decision.

Legal: I think that we can all understand the legal issues. There is the question of ownership and the fear that we won't win the account, and worse, we'll see our brilliant ideas being used months down the road by another agency. Legal rights aside, I am not sure that I can remember an agency ever suing a client for giving their ideas away to another agency. I am sure that this has been considered. But legal action hasn't been taken for all sorts of obvious reasons including how to prove the theft and an agency's desire not to look overly litigious to the broader marketplace.

Note: See my interview on intellectual property with legal expert Sharon Toerek on page 180.

Emotion: In my experience, agency emotions often rule the do or not do spec decision. Some of the questions we ask ourselves include:

- Is the client asking for free ideas, *and* do we think that this is the right way for them to act in this pitch?

- Do we think we can win the account if we do *not* do spec work?

- Do we have an idea so fantastic that we just have to work it up and present it?

- Do we think we need to do spec to demonstrate our passion and interest?

- Do we think that the other agencies will do spec work, and if we don't, we'll lose?

- Do we need this account so badly that we have to do whatever it takes and not worry about the consequences? These consequences include the fact that working on spec can hurt agency morale, eats into existing client work, and means that we may need to hire freelancers.

Tip:

Here is one way to look at the spec work question. Think of it as The Good, The Bad, And The Ugly.

The Good: In my personal experience, the odds of winning the account were greatly improved when we did spec work. The reason why is simple. I have been blessed to work with really good creative talent that wanted to do spec work to prove our excellence. My Citrus partner and ECD Kevin Archer helped us win over 50% of our major pitches. There is no question that his work, passion, and sincere presentation style won accounts. I can't tell if we would have won without his creative group's spec work. But I do know that it worked magic.

The Bad: As I said earlier, spec work can create ill will at the agency. It eats us up, has a high cost, and takes away our attention from current clients. If you are wavering at all, don't do it. Wavering probably means that you could be about to do a half-assed job.

The Ugly: Back to the process issue. You should only do spec work if you have the time to do research and generate the insights necessary to create a smart creative brief that will drive pitch winning creative solutions. Throwing creative spaghetti against the client's wall while hoping that one or more random ideas stick is a very lame and unproductive business process. If you don't have the time or energy to build the strategic support for the spec work, then there is a good chance that your creative solutions won't win you anything.

Part Three: Presentation Prep

As I stated in the introduction, there are many types of pitches. Some are sophisticated, and some might seem like the minor leagues. It does not matter if this is a pitch that you really really want to win. Wanting isn't enough. To win the pitch, you will need to be perfect.

The Presentation Outline

Now that you have a good, hopefully perfect, idea of what it will take to win, you will need to plot out your presentation using an outline and master script. You will have 'nice to have' and 'must have', points to make. You have a time limit so use the outline to plan your 'must haves' and put what doesn't fit into your precious presentation time limits in the leave behind. Make sure you reference your leave behind document more than once during your presentation so that it has direct value and becomes a must read.

Virtually all of the presentation gurus tell us to think of presentation elements as acts in a play. You will need to balance how you present the facts that the clients must hear with your unique vision. If you think of the presentation as acts, then you can introduce each act, build interest, and deliver your key points.

Tip:

One of the most insightful perspectives on presentation dynamics is in the best-selling presentation book *Resonate* by Nancy Duarte. Duarte uses a graphical tracking system called *sparklines* to visually track a presentation's flow and major points. I urge you to look at Duarte's sparklines examples including how Steve Jobs introduced the iPhone and how Mozart used the three-part sonata form for his Eine kleine Nachmusik.

Watch Nancy's TEDx video that presents her sparklines analysis of how Steve Jobs introduced the iPhone. Watch for what she views as Job's top four dramatic techniques: repeatable sound bites, shocking statistics, evocative visuals, and memorable dramatization. I also suggest that you have your pitch team watch Jobs' iPhone presentation. This is as good as it gets and is great pre-pitch stimuli.

Note: See Nancy's interview on chemistry and presentation dynamics in Chapter Six.

Be A Clock Slave

Be a slave to the clock. Go in thinking that no matter how brilliant you are, the client will still stand up and head out the door when the meeting is over. If you still need ten minutes to go to deliver your big point, well, tough luck. Make sure you know how long you have, and plan your presentation accordingly.

Even if you believe that you've planned every minute, there is a good chance that things will take longer than you think. If you have one hour, plan a forty-five minute presentation. If you have two hours, plan for one and a half. There are more chances than not that you will need more time than you planned for. Ending a presentation because you ran out of time, um, what's the right word? Sucks. I know it. I've been there and can clearly remember that there were times in the middle of a presentation when I started to worry that we were about to go over the time limit. This is bad because you just killed your chances to make all of your points, or you had to rush through them. Rushing will make you look like you don't do planning and deadlines very well. Worse, you will look very scattered. This can be a trust busting moment.

One more point. Having some air in your presentation is a good thing. No client will ever bitch that you didn't fill up every minute with your super detailed PowerPoint presentation that includes every powerful creative idea your agency has ever had.

Tip:

Make sure that the leader has a stopwatch to track the presentation. Smartphone timers are a bit less intrusive.

Have some preplanned hand signals to signal when a speaker's time is running out. As simple as it sounds, pulling on an ear should help you tell your media director that going on about Twitter's latest ad unit is about to ruin your meeting's timing. The ear thing could help your art director to hold back and not go ad lib with a long story about his favorite Brazilian TV shoot.

Think Flow

We can learn a lot from Nancy Duarte's sparklines analysis of Steve Jobs. However, I suspect that you might be thinking that channeling a new Apple product launch with the dramatic reveal of the first ever iPad might not directly relate to an agency pitch about advertising the essence of Widgets. An advertising agency new business pitch most likely does not have an earth-moving climax. But let's get past that. For another path to channel, consider Aristotle.

Aristotle, apparently one of the earlier presentation coaches, is credited with developing the three act structure and advising Greek scriptwriters to, *"Tell them what you are going to tell them, tell them, then tell them what you told them."*

Tell them what you are going to tell them. Tell them what you want to say and what they want to hear from you. This will set up your major points and will let the client know that you have your act together.

Tell them. In this section you'll tell them that you understand their needs, that you have the experience to meet these needs, and that you have proof that you can deliver. Think of this as the content section.

Tell them what you told them. I consider this the support section. You will reiterate your major points, support these points with clear rationale, and you will nail your pitch with conviction and enthusiasm.

The Three parts:

Here is a deeper look at what I think are the three primary acts of a winning pitch. Not all of the individual elements are required since every client request is different, but for the most part, not thinking through your script from the client's perspective will lower your odds.

Caveat: There is no single method for how to script presentation flow. We are in a creative industry where our clients expect us to look and act creatively. So take my perspective on flow as a starting point. My bottom-line however, is that you need to be very conscious about your script, actors, and stagecraft.

The Opening:

First impressions are critical. Know how you will grab the audience's attention at the start. What might be the one thing you say within the first couple of minutes – maybe even seconds – that will build trust and interest… and set you well apart from the preceding or following agency?

Do you want to introduce everyone at once? How do you ask the client to introduce their team? Do you do this casually or more formally as part of the scripted presentation? Manage these interpersonal moments. Don't fumble introductions or take too much time. My take is the quicker the better. Plan out this early chemistry building moment. The first few moments are critical.

Tell your audience what you plan to do in the meeting and that you understand that there is a time limit. Try to take any client questions relating to the way you will manage the presentation off the table. TED conference speakers and the audience all know that the presentation won't go over 18 minutes. This helps to frame the experience for the speaker and the audience.

The Middle:

Storytelling is always a good way to move from introductions to the main part of the presentation. Stories do all of those wonderful things that stories do (they frame the conversation, they are memorable, they are friendly), and they can act as a metaphor for your presentation theme. You have a theme that will create differentiation, right? I think that there is an opportunity to weave a story into your discussion of any research and insights you have. Why not tell the story of why and how you did the research itself. This could provide a personal look at how your agency thinks and manages process.

If your presentation needs to have a credentials section, tailor it to match the client's needs. There can't be anything more boring than hearing an agency CEO ramble on too long about his history or the agency's size, skills, and track record. Efficiently deliver your credentials so they *directly* match up with the client's business objectives and issues, and you will frame your skills and history in a way that nails the sale.

Make sure that you answer all of the client's primary questions. If you can't for timing reasons, let them know that you have all of the answers in the leave behind.

Activate the client's participation in the presentation. Talking *at* rather than *with* a group of clients for an hour or two is not a way to build a relationship. Yes, I know that some clients will sit mute and stone-faced regardless of how many pearls you put before them. Some actually think that this is a good idea. You will just have to read the room, pick your moments, and then pull out your best interpersonal skills.

Know when you need to build in images to make your major points or really hammer your primary insights. *Show* can be more important than *tell* especially by the mid-point when your audience's attention might be flagging.

In fact, think about when the audience might begin to fade no matter how effervescent your presentation is. This is where your agency's impartial pitch critic should have helped you plan accordingly. I'll talk about this important role later. Make sure that your critic is looking ahead for any boredom or fatigue inducing moments when they critique your presentation.

The Close:

Go back to Aristotle. Your close should restate your major points and meld the rational (make sure you made your key points) with the emotional (this is a chemistry moment). Leave them wanting more. More is usually a good thing.

Tip:

I am using the word 'flow' to help you plan your presentation. I am really talking about the S-Word – Sales. Your presentation needs to flow like an elegant sales script.

It's Sales Stupid

An agency pitch is a sales pitch. Sounds obvious, right? The problem is that 'sales' is a dirty word at some 'creative' agencies. If you think that I am overstating this, take a look at a few agency websites, and ask yourself if they are designed to be high-octane sales experiences that drive leads or just well designed agency brochures.

A discussion of how to use the science of salesmanship in an agency presentation could fill a book. I'll be brief and hit what I think are the most effective techniques we can learn from the masters of salesmanship. Allow me a brief detour first.

I left advertising in 1995 to put a group of New Jersey newspapers online for Advance Internet (the digital newspaper arm of the Newhouse media group – you know them as the owner of Condé Nast). In addition to inventing New Jersey Online's digital newspaper editorial persona, we also had to build an early online sales program that included the design of new advertising units and a sales pitch for this new Internet platform. To help me, Advance brought in Jim Hagaman, one of the savviest media sales people I had ever met.

Within a few days, I had gone from thinking that I knew how to sell, to jettisoning much that I had learned, to watching a master actually make sales in the nascent Internet marketplace. Much of what you see below came from Jim.

One of his more interesting sales insights came when I said that we needed to go pitch New Jersey Online to New York advertising agencies. He said, whoa boy. In his experience, agencies always mucked up the sale. They wanted to put their ownership stamp on the sales message, usually got the details wrong, and always slowed down the process. He said that we were going directly to the clients to explain the benefits of digital media. As I eventually witnessed, he was right.

Actually, here is one more super insightful story that will introduce my next point, which I admit might be a "duh" for some of you.

> You have to understand your client's mindset, needs, pain points, rationale, and emotional motivations before you can ever craft an effective sales pitch.

I learned this lesson at my first agency pitch. I figured I'd start with my ex, Saatchi & Saatchi New York. I knew the agency inside and out and had worked with their Executive Media Director Allen Banks for years. My pitch included a hockey puck graph of projected Internet usage and a discussion of digital advertising that touted our newfound ability to track how website visitors viewed and interacted with online advertising. Was Allen smiling? No. His reaction? *"Are you f*cking kidding me? We have made a fortune not really knowing how, when and for how long consumers have been looking at our ads. I manage hundreds of millions in advertising media placement. Knowing how much of it doesn't work will kill our golden goose."* My point in telling you this story is that I didn't think through Allen's motivations before I delivered my early online sales pitch. By the way, he was right. The Internet sure seems like it killed some parts of the golden advertising goose.

More advice from the world of sales.

Think like the client. The presentation must be written from the client's perspective. What are they asking for, and what do they need *and* want to hear? You want to win *them* over, not your colleagues. This is the key reason why you have to learn about the individual clients before you ever meet them.

Involve them. Don't make the presentation one-sided. Try to involve the client in a discussion. You might be able to motivate the stone-faced clients by asking them a few questions at the right time.

Answer *their* questions. If the client has specific questions, make sure you answer them and confirm with them that you have. Think all agencies do this? I know for a fact that they don't. Sometimes in the heat of the pitch, agency presenters will consciously or unconsciously deflect the client's question so that they can get on with their scripted presentation. This can be a major lost opportunity for dialog and might put off the client.

Deliver value. The client has invited you into their world. Return the favor by giving them something of value in return. In most cases, this might be a serious insight or a creative solution. This is your chance to demonstrate why this client couldn't possibly live without you.

Be dynamic. Clients want agencies that are passionate about their work and ideas. Show your passion, and find a way to show passion for the client's brand and/or quest. You might want to consider actually asking for the job. Jim taught me that leaving the room without a sense of a prospect's interest and next steps was, hmmm, nuts.

Be different. The other agencies that are pitching are good, smart and could probably do the job. You have one chance to look and sound different. Think very hard about how you will stand out from the pack.

Tip:

I suggest that you read a couple of books or blogs on sales techniques. You will benefit from the learning and could get psyched by a sales master's energy. These are serious sales guys, and they are selling you on *their* sales pitch. Pay attention.

If you need some sight and sound stimulation, revisit Mamet's Glengarry Glen Ross. Need a line to keep in the back of your head? Watch Alec Baldwin hammer home, *"A-B-C. A-Always B-Be C-Closing. Always be closing."* Sure, it's a 1980's approach and just might freak out some of your more sensitive colleagues, but the idea of ABC will get those sales juices flowing.

I have a list of my favorite sales books in the online Playbook.

KISS

Keep it Simple Stupid works.

A jam-packed presentation loaded with agency credentials, too many ideas, too many presenters and a dozen creative executions that cover every issue the client has or might ever have in their lifetime, will not help you win. The client will be overwhelmed, and you won't be able to build personal rapport. The client, especially the client that has to sit through four other agency presentations, could even go into deep REM sleep. I have seen it happen.

Worse, they won't leave the room hearing or remembering your USP (Unique Selling Proposition). Think of it this way: CMO + REM + No USP = No Sale.

I truly want to think that an agency could walk into a pitch meeting room and just present one concise insight that leads to one brilliant advertising idea that leads to one mind-blowing execution that leads to the client decision maker saying "I love you, I need you, where's the contract?" But I am not that crazy. Or am I?

Keep these KISS Moments in mind.

Lincoln's Gettysburg Address was only 272 words long.

Churchill is famously known for his request for brevity in cabinet documents.

M&C Saatchi recognizes that in today's digital-overload world where people have the attention span of butterflies, getting even one point across and being remembered for it is golden. In M&C Saatchi parlance, 'Brutal Simplicity' rules.

Conversely, we've all sat through State Of The Union addresses that are so jam-packed that we don't remember anything. Clinton's 2000 speech was 2 hours, 28 minutes and 49 seconds long. What do you remember him saying that night?

Tip:

Of course you can use all the time the client has given you to deliver your presentation. But that does not mean that you need to overwhelm them with detail.

Think like Martin Luther King. His *I Have A Dream* speech was only 17 minutes long and included the key (as in easy to remember) line *"I have a dream."* Johnny Cochrane knew this when he helped O.J. Simpson with the line, *"If it doesn't fit, you must acquit."*

You are in advertising and study culture. Think like a preacher, lawyer or even a skilled headline copywriter. Think of the power of Apple's simple tagline that delivers the highly competitive message: *"Think Different"*.

WOW!

Being what I call 'Wowerful' isn't a new idea, but many agencies don't do it. So here you go. Every presentation must include Wow! Moments. What's a good number? Two? OK, maybe three at most.

Hopefully, your Wow!s started at the beginning of the agency search process. You created brand distinction for your agency via surprising insights in your RFP response. You wanted the client to start to think very early, *"Wow, these guys are different, better, smarter, more fun – I want them."* Build on this. Presentation Wow!s can be that moment when the client makes the decision that they can't live without you.

Tip:

Strategically schedule the delivery of your precious Wow!s. Use them to nail major points, to surprise, to engage with individual team members, and to keep the client awake.

I don't want to dwell on another worst-case scenario. But imagine that you are the fourth agency to present. It's 4PM on a Friday, and the client has already sat through three two-hour agency pitches. I don't care if you are Tracy Wong, Susan Credle, or Alex Bogusky. This client is getting fried, and your brilliant rationale might fall on deaf ears. It is time to dial things up, and use a powerful strategic Wow! to grab their attention, deliver your most motivating point, and nail your pitch.

Chutzpah and BHAGS

Why not go a step further, and wrap that Wow! in a chutzpah sandwich.

Just in case you haven't seen any Woody Allen movies, chutzpah is the Yiddish word for confidence, courage, and audacity. Here are two famous Chutzpah Moments:

A man is up in court for killing his mother and father… he pleads to the court for leniency… because he is an orphan.

Or, from Guy Kawasaki: "Chutzpah is calling up tech support to report a bug in your pirated software."

What is pitch chutzpah you ask? In the world of agency pitches, I'll take the definition a bit further and just say it means that you have cojones – figuratively speaking, that is.

Most agency presentations don't. Most are look alike, sound alike, and act *like* recitations. OK, this might be another overstatement. But there can be no question that the great majority of agency pitches play it safe and don't demonstrate any go-for-it "I am going to sound different" antics. By fearing differentiation, they might be setting themselves up for a loss.

Every pitch is its own beast, and it is difficult to generalize. But I suggest that you add BHAG's or Big Hairy Audacious Goals (C/O Jim Collins and Jerry Porras) to your pitch in addition to your must-have information. In the words of that great Italian-American salesman Vito Corleone, *"Make the client an offer they can't refuse."* In this case it might be a BHAG offer wrapped in a chutzpah sandwich. How often do we get to create a Vito and Woody love child?

Oh, a bit of warning, chutzpah does have its limits. Keep away from beating any baby seals.

Who's In The Room?

In the best of all possible worlds, the smart transparent client has told you who from their side will be in the presentation room. If this is the case, do your homework. There is no reason that you should ever walk into a presentation without knowing the history of every client that will be judging your presentation. Use your digital tools: the client's website, search engines, LinkedIn, industry contacts, Twitter, Facebook, YouTube, alumnae websites, etc.

No more blind dates.

I love to tell digital natives that there was once a social event called the blind date. The blind date was a date where a mutual friend acted as a matchmaker to set you up with their friend. This event usually started with *"I have the perfect person for you."* Back in those pre-Facebook, Tinder and Google days, it meant that the first time I ever saw my blind date's face was when she opened up her front door. Knock, knock, *hello*. Blind dates were cool (well, some of the time). But they are now a thing of the past. Today's client meeting should never be like a blind date. No one, including your prospective clients, should ever be a total stranger.

Tip:

LinkedIn is clearly one of the best client research tools. Sure, you will have scoped out the client team's LinkedIn profiles. I have another angle that I think can be more revealing than just studying a fact-based profile or how others recommend the individual clients.

To gain a deeper, more revealing understanding of the individual client's personality, motivations, and interests (think hot-buttons), examine how the client herself recommends others. This reverse angle will give you direct insight into how *they* think and what *they* value.

Let's pretend that you are going to pitch KIA and know that a key decision maker is Kia's EVP Michael Sprague. Here is an example of this type of reverse engineering that will help you get to know Michael – from the inside out. Below is a LinkedIn recommendation made by Michael for his colleague David Greenberg, who Michael worked with at Mazda. This is Michael talking about David with his personal insights highlighted below:

> *"David is one of the most **passionate and innovative marketers** in the business. David's **knowledge and insights into the brand strategy process** (vision, segmentation, target customer, positioning, etc...) enabled him to lead a global team in the development of Mazda's global brand positioning centered around "Zoom-Zoom". Having worked for David in Japan, I witnessed how he **easily adapts** to his environment, working **cross-functionally and cross-culturally**. I highly recommend David."*

By using this reverse engineering, I found at least four revealing personal attributes for Michael based on his recommendation, in his voice, of his colleague David. We see that Michael values strategic thinking, passion, innovation, and cross-management prowess. This can be powerful learning for how you craft your presentation's key points to sync with Michael's own hot buttons.

Presenter Chemistry, Please

Assuming that your presentation, including your information and your strategic and creative solutions are smart and compelling, the next most important factor in how the client will judge you is…

Personal chemistry.

Chemistry may seem like an intangible best left to fate. It's not. You know which of your agency people have charisma, the ability to connect, and deliver compelling presentations. You need to lead with these folks.

Including poor presenters because they wrote the strategy, media plan, the ads, programmed the code, stayed up nights working on the pitch, or a much worse reason, *it's their turn to pitch*, is a big mistake. Believe me, I've made the error of fielding the wrong team and paid for it by having to take the "We loved what you presented but didn't really click with the red headed guy on your team. Sorry." call from the client.

As you will see in my interviews with agency search consultants, many agencies fail at looking like *they* have positive interpersonal relationships. If agency team members don't look like a cohesive unit, how could they work well with the client? There are even large agency network pitches where the client gets to see agency people from different offices meet each other for the first time. "Hi, I'm Tom from our Chicago office, here's my card." This certainly doesn't breed a sense of client security.

Tip:

Use your best presenters only, please. There really aren't any good excuses because showing up with poor presenters will virtually guarantee that you will come in "second".

The only caveat I see is that some clients ask that their day-to-day team be in the presentation. If these people are not good presenters, then you better work hard and fast to quickly help them hone their skills with some finely tuned pointers to help them get comfortable. Better yet, a smart agency won't wait for the drama of an impending pitch to start to do some in-house presentation training. Even many savvy TED presenters start preparing how to present one year ahead of their TED Talk.

Pitching ideas is done everyday at a busy agency. Learning how to pitch and present should be a skill nurtured across the agency.

Listen Up

Man, when I know I am going to present to a prospective client, I want to really dazzle them with my words.

I really love what I have to say.

I want my audience to lean in and listen to all of my stellar pearls of wisdom. Damn I'm good!

Because of my self-love, I sometimes forget that I should be leaning in too. Listening is a wonderful gift that you can give to your audience. A gift that will result in them liking you for liking them. And isn't liking you what you want them to do?

Tip:

Make sure that you are conscious about the act of listening. This may be easier said than done. But just do it, and get used to doing it every day. Early in my career I was trained in the art of 'active listening'. Active listening makes sure that the person doing the talking knows via your eye contact, body language, and the use of follow up questions that you are paying attention to *their* fabulous pearls of wisdom.

Here is a simple active listening training exercise I do at cocktail parties.

Sometimes when someone is talking to me, my attention starts to wander and I begin to think about the story *I* want to tell them. At this point, I have stopped listening. To correct this, I tell myself that I already know what I know, but I don't know what they are about to say. Spending my time retelling my stories may massage my ego, but not my brain.

Keep Your Numbers Low

Is there a perfect number of presenters? No. Must everyone in the room have a roll to play? Yes.

That said, I am going to go with the *less is more* approach on how many agency people to have in the room. You will have to think very hard about each presenter's role, how the agency needs to look (as in how to balance looking resourceful while looking efficient), how the presenters relate to each other, diversity in roles and gender, and what the client is specifically looking for from your agency. If they want to see members of the team that will actually work on their account you will need to address this request.

In most cases, clients are looking for a cost-effective agency. This means that if you look bulked up and expensive because you are showing up with lots of people, the client might think that you are inefficient or worse, that you are going to load up their billable hours.

It's a ratio game. You also need to consider how many clients will be in the room. Coming in with an overwhelming and overpowering gang is a losing proposition. This is another reason why you need to get an early understanding of how many clients will be attending the presentation.

Tip:

A critical point: having too many people in the room will dilute your chance to build the interpersonal chemistry that wins pitches. Remember one of my favorite pitch mistakes:

Use your numbers to crowd the room and destroy any opportunity to build
person-to-person chemistry. Make your presentation like dating quintuplets.

The relationship that you nurture with the client is partially due to how they perceive your own interpersonal chemistry. Clients want to work with a team that looks like they like and work well with each other. Your rehearsals will go a long way towards managing how your team members relate.

Be Gentle

You want the right people to be in the actual presentation, but you also need to have a fully invested team to craft, write, and produce the presentation itself. Some agency staff will be demotivated by having to work nights while knowing that they will be left at the agency's curb on the day of the presentation. You must manage this. This is where your ego massage skills come in.

Being 100% upfront and strategic about who will be on the team bus, and who will be left at home, early in the pitch development process is the only way to accomplish the task of keeping everyone invested. Be honest about the need to keep the numbers down, that there are certain roles that must be filled, that everyone presenting must give great stand-up, and that the agency pitch team has to be designed to win the business.

Tip:

If a key player is not in the presentation because of their lack of presentation skills, then take the time after the heat of the pitch to get them some training so they are ready for the next pitch. That alone will help keep their morale high and will signal the importance of presentation skills development to your entire organization.

When I started in the ad business, my agency had all of their AE's take presentation skills training. This training was designed to help us sell our work and eventually, play a role on the agency's pitch team. This was a great investment then, and it doesn't have to cost as much today. Here's an inexpensive idea: use your mobile phone to record your colleagues presenting and then do an assessment. Point out their "ums" and "you knows" so they will leave them well behind. Your staff wants to hone their skills. This is a win for them and for you. Get ahead of your next pitch. Do this next month.

Role Playing

Once you have your presentation team set, you need to make sure that you use each person correctly. Everyone must have a clear role to play. Each person's part must be additive to the total presentation.

Every pitch and required cast of characters is different based on what the client is asking to see and your needs assessment. But there is a set of usual suspects. Determine which of these team member types will be needed to deliver your sales message, and yes, keep your numbers in check. Here are some of the usual players.

The Boss. Including the agency CEO always depends on agency size, their potential role on the account, and if they are a killer presenter. I think that if the CEO is in the room, they should play a larger strategic role than just MC. A cardboard Mr. Smiles doesn't cut it.

The Creative Director. Most clients are buying your creativity. The CD usually shows up with a way to frame your insights and will demonstrate the passion and energy of the agency.

The Strategist. After creativity, clients look for strategic thinking. They need a strategic agency that will help them understand both their market and customers and to find the message hooks that will drive market leadership. It is the strategist's job, one of the great roles of the English Account Planner world, to sell in the agency's strategic thinking and make the agency look… smart. If the Strategist has a proper British accent, so much the better. If you don't have a dedicated strategist, then position someone as Ms. Strategy.

The Media Director (or in today's world) the Digital, or Social Media Strategist. The media universe is complex and getting more complex on a daily basis. Clients are like deer in the headlights, and they know it – even big brands like P&G. Show up with someone that can begin to demonstrate how to solve the traditional, social, and mobile media riddle based on the client's specific business issues. Be careful of not being too blue-sky.

The Analyst. Quant jock, master of analytics, director of metrics, or ROI Queen. Whatever you call this person, it is their role to prove to the client that you understand their business objectives and the importance of analytics and measurement to the client's success. Clients need to know that you value ROI as much as they do. Maybe even more. Chief Data Officer or CDO anyone?

The Account Director. Clients want to see who they will be dealing with on a daily basis. This can be your toughest cast member challenge. Your seasoned Account Supervisor should do a great job. However, will your newbie AE look sharp, knowledgeable, and nail their presentation? This person may need the most prep time. Clients can excuse the nerdiness of a quant jock, but the AE better be able to communicate.

Tip:

Your Presentation Creative Brief should help you know exactly who will need to be in the presentation. Base this decision on the client's requests, their needs (creative super stars or business partners), an assessment of their personality, and what you really think it will take to win, while yes, keeping those numbers down. Bring on people that can deliver a bit of chutzpah. Navel gazing is not a good thing. Here is its definition: *"self-indulgent or excessive contemplation of oneself or a single issue, at the expense of a wider view."*

The Impartial Critic

As the pitch leader, you will get in so deep that chances are very good you will lose a degree of objectivity in addition to being stressed out. Pick presentation development stages where you seek the opinion and advice of a smart third-party. Seek out a merciless critic, and get their input when you have the time to make revisions. I know from experience that this works. I got to stand in as an impartial critic to review pitches across the Saatchi network, and I've used impartial critics myself to review my own agency's presentations.

Tip:

Here is a win-win idea. Need an impartial critic? Go past your agency friends and bring in a friendly client to review your presentation. They will show up with a very different perspective than your team or in-house critic.

The more I think about this, the smarter this idea sounds. I bet that a savvy client might relish the idea of seeing how an agency makes its presentation sausages and will feel respected for being asked to help. This process kills two birds by getting a valuable objective perspective while building greater trust with your current client.

Body Language

If we agree that interpersonal chemistry is a critical component in agency selection, then we better get out our test tubes.

One experiment that you don't want to run in the face-to-face meeting is how to manage, use, and read body language. This isn't new territory for most agency people as we spend a fair amount of time trying to decipher our current client's body language in daily strategy and creative meetings. It really is amazing to see the difference between a client that leans in and one that folds their arms, crosses their legs, and leans back.

Albert Mehrabian is the Professor Emeritus of Psychology at UCLA and is well known for his study of verbal and non-verbal communication. According to Mehrabian's 3 V's of Communication, visual cues rule. Here's his take on the three elements in face-to-face communication:

Verbal – words, content – 7%

Vocal – tone, pitch, intonation – 38%

Visual – body language, facial expression, gestures – 55%

Wow, content only gets 7%!?

I was a bit dumbfounded when I first saw this verbal, vocal, and visual breakdown. Is it possible that non-verbal communication is the essential ingredient of a successful presentation? Well no. And, that isn't what Mr. Mehrabian is saying. Here is how a sage Wikipedian reports on Mehrabian's conclusions.

> *"It is not the case that non-verbal elements in all senses convey the bulk of the message, even though this is how his conclusions are sometimes misinterpreted. For instance, when delivering a lecture or presentation, the textual content of the lecture is delivered entirely verbally, but the non-verbal cues are very important in conveying the speaker's attitude towards what they are saying, notably their belief or conviction."*

Ah, the demonstration of *"belief or conviction"*. I think that this point is very important because we know that there can be an element of distrust in how some clients in the room might view an advertising agency presentation – *"Oh, they will say anything to win the account; they are ad guys after all."*

I think that some of this thinking comes from the nature of our presenting the intangible magic of advertising. A sense of disbelief is part of being on the buyer end of any somewhat subjective sales pitch. Therefore, we need to pay close attention to our non-verbal cues.

Playing to the intangibles of body language require you to play two roles.

1. The first is the role of observer. Is the client leaning in? Are they making eye contact or looking around the room or at their papers? How are they holding their arms (hopefully, not folded in front of them)? Are they fidgeting? Better, are they nodding in agreement, and are they taking notes?

   Make sure that your team understands how to read the important positive and negative 'tells'. Everyone should think like a poker player. If you need some extra stimulus on how to read the room, watch David Mamet's great gambling movie *House of Games*.

2. Your other role is to be aware of your own body language, and make sure that your team is fully conscious of how *they* deliver their body language. Personally, I have always focused on my breathing, posture, and the position of my hands, head and eyes. I remind myself to go to an out-of-body view of how I might be perceived during the presentation. Self-awareness during the pitch is all-important.

We should want to look relaxed and stand straight. In this case, you also need to beware of looking too cool, or looking like the shifty poker players you see on TV who often want to demonstrate power by acting aloof. Rather, lean in like President Obama or Sean Hannity (hey, I am an equal opportunity viewer). Look like you believe in what you are saying and that you are confident.

Much of your conscious performance will be driven by your rehearsals which will make you familiar with your ideas, words, tone, pace, and body position. It is ok to critique each other during the rehearsal. Better that you point out a colleague's wandering eye problem than have the client experience it later.

Tip:

Be very conscious of your surroundings.

Make sure that you actively read the room. Pay attention to your audience, listen closely to their comments for clues, and note their posture. Be prepared to make subtle adjustments to your presentation based on what you are seeing. I have been in pitches where I know that my colleague is failing by watching the audience's reaction. In a worse case scenario, the speaker isn't paying attention to his audience – he is just trying to deliver his lines and get though his section. Bad move for him and for you. All of your presenters must be aware of how they are being received and make adjustments. Have a set of visual codes to alert your colleagues about any body language fails. You might want to have your impartial critic act disinterested in your rehearsal just for practice.

Rehearse. Rehearse. But.

You know that building chemistry with the client can win you the business. You know that looking professional and like a well-oiled team will help you win. You know that you can't win without knowing your material. You know that you won't win if you don't have an agency story to weave or some Wow!'s. You know that leaning in works.

You know this.

You also know that the only way to deliver your message, know each other's roles, and how your individual styles will fit together is to rehearse. Make sure that the schedule discussed earlier includes having at least two, *at least two*, full-team rehearsals. And make sure that your impartial critic is in the room.

Making multiple rehearsals happen is your job as team leader. This responsibility falls firmly on your shoulders. You have to think that failing to rehearse will lead to failure.

Tip:

I just gotta hammer this one home… Rehearsals must be viewed as a critical element of creating a winning pitch and must built into your timetable. They cannot be an afterthought that gets left out of the process because you ran out of time. Every presentation expert tells you that you need to Rehearse. Rehearse. Rehearse.

In this case, you don't have to just take my word for it. Take *everyone's* word and do it.

But…

Yes, there is a but. Laura Bajkowski of Bajkowski + Partners, a leading agency search consultancy, points out that agencies can rehearse way too much.

> *"… agencies cram a lot of content in and rehearse it to death to determine how much faster they need to talk. And they seem to overlook how to draw the clients into the process."*

This is a critical point. Your presentation must not be so over rehearsed that it becomes an unyielding one-way recitation. Reading from a script and not paying attention to the audience is boring, and frankly can be insulting. Recitations sans eye contact surely don't make many friends.

Part Four: The Delivery

Presentation Tools

In an earlier chapter, I mentioned that one of the reasons that Dancer Fitzgerald Sample won the Western Union Easylink account way back in the 1980's was because we dazzled the client with our use of a wall of syncopated slide projectors that delivered our powerful insights and ideas. The projectors were, in fact, dazzling. But just as importantly, they melded with the client's technology mindset, they supported our messaging, they were different, and they were easy to use because we presented at our agency.

Allow me to break this down. I think that how you select your presentation system is a very strategic decision.

Dazzle. It's getting harder to dazzle these days. We all have access to technology, and our creative and production teams know all about the latest presentation platforms. With that in mind, I think that dazzle does not have to mean using the latest digital toolset. It could mean how you use paper, Fom-Cor Board, or an easel. Think like a magician. Maybe all you need is to pull your brilliant ideas out of a hat.

If you need one thought to galvanize this point: the client is in the room to hear your message, not to see your technology. Here are some thought starters.

Client-Think Design. Western Union viewed themselves as a technology company. We chose a presentation system that we knew would make us look like we were into technology. Match your presentation tools to the client's mind-set. Do they really need a high-tech approach? Maybe they are the type who just needs a presentation board that delivers the Big Hairy Audacious Goal in a single sentence.

If I had been the BMW CMO, I would have dug, understood, and loved New York's Ammirati & Puris when they presented the tag line, "The Ultimate Driving Machine". It was so freakin' right-on that it could have been presented on a cocktail napkin. Hmm, why not present your big idea on a napkin? Tell the client that your account planner discovered the big idea while eating a burrito. Now that could be a good story.

Be Different. Easier said than done. But it can be done. My agency once presented to save a Nike account using a very early form of a scrolling horizontal website as our presentation tool. Why did we use this technique? We knew that our presentation had to sync with the Internet to show competitive digital marketing campaigns and we didn't want to click back and forth from PowerPoint to a browser. It looked cool, met our needs, and we, in fact, stood out.

Don't kill yourself. There was no way that we could have pulled off our multi-screen projector presentation anywhere but at our own offices. We pulled off the interactive Nike presentation because we were familiar with their conference rooms. Today, relying on a client's untested Internet service can be a mistake. Don't set yourself up for technological defeat if you don't know the details of the room you are pitching in. In some cases subscribing to KISS is the best way to go. Let your Fom-Cor ideas rule. Keep It Simple Stupid.

Which system?

Now that you know the details of the venue and your presentation theme, it's time to pick a presentation system. Here are some of the old stand-bys, and latest digital tools. Of course, you could always just use some boards. As you will see later in my interview with Tony Mikes, the agency that used simple presentation boards won the National Aquarium account.

PowerPoint. Microsoft introduced PowerPoint in 1990. 1990! Before that we were somewhat limited to boards, presentation books, overhead projectors, and slides.

At its birth, PowerPoint was a Godsend (well, maybe – it was created by Microsoft engineers not designers). Unfortunately, over the years, the ease of using PowerPoint has led to 'Death by PowerPoint' and 'PowerPoint Hell'. According to a 2001 New Yorker article, Microsoft reported that there were over 30,000,000 PowerPoint presentations given every day. Most are lame. But don't blame PowerPoint. It would be like blaming your car for your speeding ticket.

We have all been tortured by the misuse of PowerPoint. If I thought that skilled presenters, even advertising agency professionals, had internalized all of the ways we screw up PowerPoint presentations, I wouldn't offer the following list. As Yogi says again and again, *"It's like Déjà vu all over again."* But it really is déjà vu, so here are my top four favorite presentation killers, which by the way, can be applied to other forms of presentations because it isn't PowerPoint that kills, it is the presenter:

1. Don't load up individual slides with lots of copy. Some people subscribe to a six-word maximum. Is there a right number? No. Just keep it tight. Lots of content is not king when delivered on a slide.

2. Don't use PowerPoint templates, wizards, or transitions. Talk about cheesy.

3. Don't bullet your audience to death. Bullet points are very unemotional.

4. Don't use lame stock images.

Here are some of today's alternatives to PowerPoint. And yes, these can be misused too.

Keynote. If you are an Apple person, use Keynote. Although it really isn't that different from PowerPoint, using keynote will make Apple-addicts feel better. That said, Keynote's interface is in fact cleaner, and it is cross-platform compatible with Apple's desktop and mobile operating systems.

Google Presentations. Google Presentations offer a simple interface and the joy of real time collaboration via the Google Drive cloud. If you want easy plus friendly, this could be for you.

Prezi. Web-based Prezi was born in 2009 and now has over 30 million users. If you want bells and whistles, Prezi might be for you. It has a 3D or zoomable interface (ZUI) that looks very different from PowerPoint. (Of course, you won't know if the agency that presented ahead of you used Prezi too.) It is collaborative and syncs with iPads and iPhones. It is today's cool kid.

Haiku Deck. Haiku Deck is less than two years old. Mashable calls it the "Instagram of pitch decks". It is a fast and easy iPad tool that lets you build a presentation quickly. TechCrunch calls it "a classic tool rethought for the mobile-first generation". Now what does that mean in the context of an agency presentation? That's up to you. But I'll file this one in the cool file.

Projeqt. Another relatively new tool, Projeqt offers a non-linear story-telling platform that is device agnostic. It combines multi-media with social media and offers full-screen or filmstrip views. It is another presentation tool that's loved by the digerati.

Tip:

Don't wait until an invitation to pitch to study the world of presentation options. Some of these tools will take some practice to get right and there will be more coming down the digital road every year.

The Room, The Food & Your Look

Where is your presentation being held?

There are generally three places you will meet: your office, the client's office, or a neutral space like a hotel conference room. Each has its challenges. I've experienced all three, and no matter where you present, it is up to you to 'own' the room and the 3D experience as much as possible.

Plan the presentation experience as you would a dinner party. Plan for a few minutes of introductions, the appetizer, main course, a bit of dessert, and then goodbyes. Your plan will have to be tailored to your meeting location and the allotted time. A laissez-faire approach to planning the meeting might kill your chances. Make sure you plan for contingencies. I've seen people show up without their Mac cable. Know what? I have.

Your Office

In most cases, your office is the best place for you to run your presentation. You own the space and can control the environment. Having the pitch at your agency gives you the opportunity to fully establish your agency brand. It also lets you efficiently show off your client work, happy smiling staff, and all of that expensive furniture. If you have knock out offices that support your agency positioning (the offices of Seattle's out-of-the-box Wexley School For

Girls agency comes immediately to mind), then your office will add points. My friends at Portland's North agency have told me that their huge open industrial space with a floating conference room has added a strong sense of credibility to their sales proposition. This comes from both an agency 'cool factor' and a sense of commitment (as in they spent some bucks) that their space provides.

Here is another good Saatchi & Saatchi London story. Once upon a time when pitching Toyota, the agency used its home court advantage by transforming its ground floor reception area into a mock Toyota showroom. It's a great literal mi casa es su casa story.

One more quick story: When I ran the Northwest Airlines account, I was asked if we had an office in Korea. I said of course (despite not knowing if we actually had one), and contacted HQ to find out that we had in fact recently purchased an agency in Seoul. I flew to Seoul a couple of days ahead of the pitch to find that it was a *rather* small office with only ten employees spread out on two floors. The agency looked empty and too small for us to rip a multinational account away from the more entrenched McCann Erickson. This would not do. The day of the pitch, I had all ten employees hang out on the first floor to greet the client and then run up to the second floor while the client was on the lift. Ta da. We instantly had a twenty-person agency ready to handle this large account.

Client's Office Or Neutral Conference Room

Clients often choose to have the presentation at or near their home base. It makes sense if the finalist agencies are in more than one city, and the client wants to reduce their travel costs and control pitch variables. While I understand the reasons that clients might select this option, I think that in most cases, by staying home, they are missing a chance to gain a better understanding of an agency's culture and vibrations. Considering how important culture and chemistry are to agency selection, not visiting each agency is a missed opportunity. However, on the flip side, there is nothing like the heat of a pitch presentation to bring out the essence of an agency regardless of where the presentation is held. In this case, a neutral space might work for the client.

Here's a great Goodby Silverstein & Partners story: According to Jon Steel in his excellent book on pitching, *Perfect Pitch*, Goodby decided that they needed to create some theater to win the 1992 video game Sega account. Although the Sega client had reserved a conference room at a Foster City hotel for the final agency presentations, the agency felt it needed a larger room for their tricked out 3D / environmental presentation. They made the move easy for the client by meeting the client at the designated conference room and politely asking them to walk across the hall to a larger kitted out video game world. Goodby & Silverstein managed to stay within the client's real estate requirements while owning the new room and delivering some serious chutzpah that helped to win the account.

My takeaway, whether you are in a home or away game, is… work to own the experience.

Orchestration

Every presentation will have its own set of meeting room variables. However, there are constants that need to be considered. Some of these may sound obvious, but the devil is always in the details. Make sure you think through all of these elements.

> **The room:** If it is your room, you are cool. If it isn't, I suggest that you find some way for you, or if the meeting is far away, a local hired-gun scout, to visit the room to take photographs, review the layout, see if there is a podium, easel, windows vs. blank walls, and check out the audio visual options. Going through this process will reduce any surprises; it will let you know what you have to bring with you, how long it will take to set up, and as an added bonus, will demonstrate your professionalism to the client ahead of the meeting.

> **The technology:** If you are in an away game then you better understand the technology requirements of your presentation room. Some clients have NASA-like conference rooms. Some look like they have equipment from 1999. You have to know the tech territory before you show up.

Do you need a projector, a monitor, cables, a sound system, etc.? You should also know how long it might take you to plug in and warm up.

Timing: I'll start with Rule No. One: be on time. But being 'on time' can mean different things in different situations. I once pitched at AT&T's New Jersey headquarters. They had what seemed like a two million square foot office building. It took at least 10 minutes to walk from reception to a conference room. If the client is giving you 90 minutes for your presentation, don't arrive on time and then use 20 of your 90 minutes to get to the room and set up. Ask if you can get into the presentation room 30 minutes ahead of the meeting.

Food: I don't like having food in one to two-hour meetings. It is a big distraction. I've experienced having a nice client bring food in to the middle of a presentation, and then I got to watch as I lost control of the meeting while the clients walked around squeezing mustard on their sandwich. If you can control food-breaks, try to eat before or after the presentation. It is more social and removes Grey Poupon from the meeting scenario.

What to wear: Hoodies work in Silicon Valley, on an MIT computer scientist, or sometimes on a tech billionaire. They don't work in pitches. Does this sound obvious? Well I don't assume anything. Have a discussion with the pitch team ahead of the meeting to try to match up your wardrobe with the objectives of the presentation and the client's culture. I pitched a few financial services clients over the years, and I always wore a suit and a tie. My creative director at least wore a jacket. Conversely, we knew we could wear jeans to a start-up pitch. We were respectful of the client's culture. Think this through. It is a part of your chemistry building effort.

Tip:

Think like an experiential marketer. A presentation is an event. How you stage-manage and what you wear tells a story. Your objective is to engage.

The Leave Behind

You will spend almost as much time thinking about what you will be leaving behind when you exit the pitch room as creating the presentation itself. I admit, the term leave behind sounds almost as lame as war room. But that's what we all call it.

Before I get to thoughts on how to develop a leave behind strategy, here is one of my favorite *leave behind* stories from Michael Keeshan, when he was the President and COO of Saatchi & Saatchi New York.

Michael was leading the pitch for the mega Burger King account. The pitch took place in a hotel conference room near the client. The client was looking for a casual setting for an early chemistry meeting with a few agencies. Michael knew that JWT would be following Saatchi into the conference room, and he decided to lighten his team's mood by punking JWT. He 'accidently' left some presentation boards with a totally crazy strategy for burger marketing in the corner of the room so JWT could 'discover' them, sneak a peek, and think that Saatchi had left some inane insights behind. He also rearranged the furniture to make the seating less congenial and more presentation-like. Playing with the head of a competitive agency is one way to leave *them* behind.

Back to today.

The agency leave behind, be it paper-based or digital, serves multiple objectives and should sync with and support your presentation.

1. The leave behind should provide detailed answers to any client questions asked in their pitch request document. It is written proof that you can follow direction.

2. If on paper, it should include multiple copies of the presentation for the client and others in their organization that might not have been in the room. How many? That's up to you but delivering a dozen bound books might be overkill and is not very environmentally sound. Believe me, clients notice things like showing up with 20 pounds of paper. I once pitched International Paper, and that was, as you might expect, a different story.

3. If you run a lean and mean presentation without the dreaded copy overkill, then the leave behind should support your key messages with greater detail. Write it as if it will be read by people that were not in the presentation.

4. Finally, and this is the big one: The leave behind should act as a physical or digital representation of the agency brand to demonstrate your creativity. You want to stand out. But be careful of looking a bit too aggressive.

5. I have one caveat. Going digital is an excellent idea, but I'd support it with something physical. A physical alert of sorts that ensures that the client knows that this *invisible* communications tool is easy to remember and find. A digital leave behind can, unfortunately, be way too ephemeral and even invisible.

One can only imagine the universe of agency leave behinds. After all, agencies know that the leave behind can be one of the key elements in their demonstration of their supreme creativity and strategic thinking. In many cases, the leave behind will be your creative team's favorite part of the pitch. Make sure you have a budget and realistic timetable for the production of this element of your pitch.

Here are some ideas as food for thought.

Don't go overboard. KISS works for leave behinds too. Do the book thing. It can be anything including a simple spiral bound book to show your frugality, a web-published book using Blurb's online service, or if you have the time, print a beautiful perfectly bound book. Impressively designed, tactile books can knock people out.

Print the presentation on fine paper and put it into a branded client-agency metal or Plexiglas binder. Check out some ideas at Binders Galore. Their products are better than their name. However, note that binders are standard agency fare. If you are going up against a large agency for a large client then think bigger, better, different. They will.

Go 3-D. Think object-oriented. How high is up? Agencies have spent tens of thousands on customized leave behinds. One well-known San Francisco agency spent over $30,000 on a customized car trunk leave behind for a national fast food account.

Food works and gets shared. How about including some of your key messages in customized fortune cookies? People like food, and they like reading their fortunes. Write funny fortunes relating to their hiring you – "Hire us and you will have many Likes." Tell your story in a series of cookies.

People are cool. Video is cool. Use the leave behind to sell your agency staff and agency personality. Why not create a simple, yet powerful video like the Marty Weiss and Friends' agency video (it's on YouTube)? I loved Marty the first time I met him via his promotional video. In fact, shouldn't you already have a compelling chemistry-building video in the can already? You know the one you use on your website and can re-edit for this presentation. Create a base video once, and you can reuse it with modification for the other ten pitches you will be in this year. You can distribute the video along with the book and have it on the pitch website.

Oh, the pitch website. Why not have a dedicated password protected pitch microsite that also works on mobile devices? Include the presentation and other materials for the client. Use a platform like Cargo to build the website. Maybe tie the website into an email program that incites the client to visit the site to see something new every day. Don't do this if you can't make the site valuable.

Deliver the leave behind on iPads. You can probably buy a used or refurbished iPad 2 for $300. Sure, this can get expensive but it could be a good reason to save a couple of thousand bucks by leaving a couple of members of a way too bloated traveling pitch team behind.

The ideas are endless. But like all other elements of the pitch… strategy must rule. That's why I did not hesitate when bringing lots of paper to International Paper.

Tip:

Duh coming. Whatever you do, don't distribute the leave behind materials until *after* you finish your pitch. Don't add a distraction to the meeting. Don't give the clients something to fondle when you want 100% of their attention. I know that you know this from your daily agency business. If you hand a client a document that supports a creative pitch too early in the meeting, they will inevitably turn to the budget section before they ever see your creative executions.

The Follow-Up

Chances are good that it has been at least a couple of months since the client or consultant first made contact. This major league pitch might have included an RFI, RFP, a kick-off meeting, phone calls, questions, and your own special strategies designed to make you look smart, passionate, and well, you fill in the blanks of what you did ahead of the big presentation.

After the presentation you graciously handed over your leave behind, smiled, hugged, and walked out. Now what? Really, now what? You could sit by the phone like a 1950's ingénue on a Friday night waiting for that call or be a bit more aggressive. But how aggressive? And how long should you take before you make contact? How passionate do you want to look, because there can be a fine line between looking passionate and desperate.

As I have said before: every pitch lives in its own little world and has its own pace. Some clients recognize that you are anxious, there is a need for speed, and that they should get back to you quickly. Some are not so caring. Or worse, after going through the pitch process, they may be revaluating their initial business objectives and requirements. Need more maybes?

Maybe the client is now wondering about what type of agency they really need. Do they want a huge agency or a specialist? Maybe a decision maker just went out of mobile range to climb K2 for three weeks. Or maybe the budget has shrunk.

Or bam! After getting to know a few new agencies, they've realized that they really love the incumbent agency.

Lots of maybes. But fear of follow-up? Get over it. I mean get over over-thinking. The deal is that you have no choice but to follow-up. You have to look like you care, a lot. Clients, good clients, respect passion. Here are my 3 follow-up rules:

1. **Do it.** Find the balance between looking very interested in working with the client and being respectful of their time. Being a nuisance does not work. Acting interested does. The other agencies will follow-up. Just do your follow up smarter.

2. **Find a value-add reason to follow-up.** Chances are good that the client asked a question in the meeting that could be the basis for a follow-up call. It is quite possible that you didn't have the time during the presentation to answer a question in detail, or you might have some new related research to impart. Maybe you held back some information, and it's now time for your pre-planned reveal.

3. **Be you.** Maintain the personality you used in the presentation. Be genuine, professional, and if you can, add some humor if appropriate.

Tip:

Don't wait till after the meeting to create a follow-up plan. Think ahead and have a follow-up insight or document at the ready. Consider embedding a preplanned reason to follow-up in your presentation. Let the client know that you will be sending them something and get it to them fast. Get it in their head that you are on the ball and are proactive.

Post-Pitch Questionnaire

A few days after the presentation, you'll be wondering where is the call. Your team will casually stop by your office with that *What's Up?* look. Your CEO will walk by fidgeting. You're getting crazed. Remember the ingénue that is sitting by the phone waiting to get asked out on a date? That's you. When the call finally comes, this is what you want to hear…

> *"Congratulations, you won our account and based on your ideas we've decided to increase the marketing budget!"*

> *"We want to immediately fly your creative, production and account teams to Brazil to produce the second TV campaign you showed us."*

What you don't want to hear…

> *"You guys did a great job but you came in second."*

Second! Why is it always second? You did your best, you nailed the presentation, and you left the room thinking that they loved you. They even gave you a gift basket. But you didn't win the account. Let's face it, shit happens. Even Ted Williams didn't bat .1000.

Ok, there could be a worse answer than "you came in second". Here is a really unfortunate post-pitch story from Frank Grady, the founder of Portland's Grady Britton.

> *"In a recent pitch, we found success right up to the final round, and were then eliminated based on a change in the client's criteria. Client Comment: "Grady Britton, we love your thinking and we love your team. You are one of the top 3 finalists, however we have decided that your agency is too small to handle our business." The elimination came after we had researched the client, the market and had developed marketing strategies and creative executions.*

Situations like this emphasize the need for a pre-pitch meeting with the prospective client, which should include a detailed question and answer session. Even with meetings and preliminary relationship development, some clients don't know what they want until after competing agencies are fully engaged – in other words, client criteria often changes as the process proceeds."

Yikes!

At the point of a rejection, you will be unhappy, deflated, exhausted and could be scratching your head. Stop scratching and rollout your post pitch questionnaire. The absolute last thing that should happen at this stage is for you to be in the dark about what just happened and to have no clue why you weren't picked. You cannot end this experience without understanding what went down.

The Post-Pitch Questionnaire #1

The first thing you need to do, and I mean first, is to go way back to the start of the agency search process and make sure that the client has agreed to provide you with an open and honest assessment of your presentation – win or lose. If the client is very professional and experienced, they will have had a search agreement that includes their commitment to a post-pitch assessment. You have just spent a bundle of time and cash, and they owe it to you. Your request for a post-pitch questionnaire will help you look professional even before the pitch.

The Post-Pitch Questionnaire #2

Your post-pitch assessment also needs to involve your agency team and its perception of the development process and the presentation. You will want to review their perspective on the development process, how it was managed, any internal issues, and a review of the presentation itself. Your people must feel free to be very honest. I didn't do an internal review after my disastrous Adidas pitch but should have because agency management needed to hear about what went wrong.

Stay In Touch

If you lost, stay in touch with the client. Unless they told you that they hate you in the post-pitch questionnaire, you should consider them a friend that might give you some business in the future. Stay in touch – gently. My agency won a state lottery account by being friendly *after* we lost the initial pitch.

Being friendly also has legs. I have actually been referred to a new client by a CMO who didn't hire my agency. The client liked us, and although he didn't think we were the perfect fit for *his* business, he thought that we might be perfect for his friend's account.

CHAPTER **6**

EXPERT OPINIONS

The Experts

I consider myself to be an expert at understanding what motivates clients, unearthing strategic insights, creating compelling presentations, pitch management, and (if you are still nodding along), I'm good at giving advice. I also know where my expertise ends and when I need the opinion and experienced perspective of an expert.

I see seven important pitch-related subjects where the perspective of an expert will add to my personal views. These include:

Understanding the client mindset
The role of agency search consultants
Working with Procurement
The art of negotiation
Agency compensation
Managing legal and intellectual property issues
Strategy development
The opinion of experienced advertising agency leaders

The Client's Perspective

At the end of phase one of my advertising career, I became a client of advertising and public relations agencies. As CEO and founder of Advance Internet's New Jersey Online from 1995 to 1999, I wanted an agency that could understand the emerging world of Internet-based news and create advertising that captured the attention of this nascent market. From 2000 to 2002, I was CEO of the natural language company ActiveBuddy. In that role, I wanted a PR resource that would make our intelligent instant messaging bots like SmarterChild famous, help us build audience, and make us look hot to prospective acquirers during the first dot-com bubble. With 16 years of agency experience, I knew what I needed from agencies to achieve my objectives, and I had a large Rolodex of agency friends.

Most advertisers looking for an agency do not. They simply do not perform enough searches to act as experienced and efficient buyers. Agencies are partially to blame for adding to client confusion by not providing a clear point of difference vs. their competitor agencies. There are over ten thousand marketing agencies. Just imagine how difficult it is to pick the right one.

Some larger clients use the services of search consultants, although this number isn't more than 10 to 15% of all major searches. Other clients use prior experience, or hopefully, do an Internet search on "how to select an advertising agency" that gets them to expert advice like the ANA/4A's "Agency Selection Briefing Guidance".

Speaking of the ANA (the Association of National Advertisers)…

INTERVIEW
Bill Duggan: Group Executive Vice President, Association of National Advertisers

Bill Duggan is the Group Executive Vice President of the Association of National Advertisers. The ANA's membership includes 590 leading companies and over 10,000 brands.

Bill is primarily responsible for the management of the ANA's portfolio of marketing and media committees, conferences, sponsorship program, and thought leadership. Prior to joining the ANA, Bill worked in account management at New York's Grey Advertising and Dancer Fitzgerald Sample.

In 2013, Bill worked with a group of ANA member CMO's and the 4A's to write the white paper "Agency Selection Briefing Guidance" which is an update of 2011's "Guidelines For Agency Search". Both of these papers represent a detailed review of the issues and best practices for the search and selection of an advertising agency. I believe that it is imperative that advertising agencies help these guidelines get broad distribution across the marketing universe. Send them to your client friends. Well, maybe send them to the clients you want.

PL: Do you have any idea what percentage of your members conduct an advertising agency search each year?

Bill: ANA would not have data on percentage of members conducting searches or the number of searches. But it's pretty clear that search activity has increased. A couple of reasons for that:

Media fragmentation: There are more new media types (e.g., social, mobile), and as a result, clients have the need for specialists in these areas. Hence more searches.

Short-term environment: The shorter longevity of the average CMO tenure has been well documented (even though it's recently been increasing). Of course, new heads of marketing often lead to searches for new agencies.

PL: Are you seeing a reduction in agency of record relationships vs. growth in project work assignments? Are these pitches different?

Bill: Absolutely more project work assignments. I could not really say if these pitches are different.

PL: What do you see as the primary issues of the agency search process that reduce the efficiency of agency selection?

Bill: I think that bad process on the marketer side undermines some searches. Marketers need to realize that there is a direct correlation between the quality of the input that they provide to agency candidates and the quality of the output from those respective agencies. Process 'worse' practices include poor briefing, limited involvement from the senior marketer, the search running for too long, clients 'floating in and out' of the process and not being part of all critical steps, clients not taking the time to visit the agency.

PL: While there is no standard search scenario, how long does this best-case process usually take?

Bill: Regarding the timetable, here's what one of our white papers says:

While searches for smaller assignments or reviews that entail a modest scope of deliverables and meetings could move more quickly, the optimal timing for the agency search process should be approximately three months:

Identification Phase: One week

RFI: Two to three weeks

RFP: Four to five weeks

Finalists: Six weeks

PL: From the outside, many agencies, especially by the time they are on the narrow finalist list, start to look alike. What criteria do you think most advertisers use to make their final decision?

Bill: I think chemistry and cultural compatibility are differentiators. Please see Appendix 3 of the ANA/4A's Guidelines for Agency Search. In many relationships, the client and agency teams spend a lot of time together. Clients need to ask themselves, *"Do I like these people and would I want to spend time (including some nights and weekends) with them?"*

PL: Does the ANA have an opinion about asking agencies to do spec creative? Shouldn't advertisers be able to determine an agency's abilities by looking at their existing portfolios and case histories?

Bill: Clients have the right to ask for spec work … and agencies have the right to say no. I think that a spec work assignment is less about the end deliverable and more about the process. The spec work assignment provides the client with insights on how an agency works and the process involved, and that can be helpful.

PL: Digital, social media, and mobile marketing require specialist skills and experience. How do advertisers select agencies that work in these complex and fast-paced marketing platforms?

Bill: I think that searches for these types of agencies are done in much the same way as searches for 'traditional' agencies. But it's a bit more important in these cases to understand how such agencies collaborate and integrate with other agencies. So those skills should be probed for in these searches.

PL: Are you seeing any macro trends in how advertisers are compensating their agencies?

Bill: Honestly, agency compensation is the topic that many marketers just can't get enough of – there is so much interest and conversation. But changes to agency comp plans have been slow to come. Performance-based compensation has been around for a while now, but we have seen indications that use is expanding. That includes use by smaller and mid-sized advertisers. Another trend is for some clients to have just one P&L, despite using multiple agencies within the same holding company.

PL: Many agency CEO's tell me that advertisers are often unwilling to tell them which other agencies are in the pitch. Why would a client choose to not to be transparent?

Bill:I think that it's fair for the agencies to know who else is 'in the game', so I honestly would not know why a client would not be transparent. I see no upside of not being transparent. And it also says something (not good!) about the client.

PL: What percentage of clients do you think use the services of professional agency search consultants? Are you seeing any trends in how search consultants are being used?

Bill: I think that a declining percentage of searches use professional agency search consultants. Since there are more searches than ever before, I would be curious to know if the actual number of searches handled by consultants has held steady or declined. Client-side procurement departments are playing increasing roles in facilitating searches. This to me has been one of the big, recent changes in search.

Some 'bad' procurement-led searches have been well publicized: RFIs repurposed from a previous sourcing role that was used for a raw material, far too many questions, especially too many questions on costs, having far too many agencies involved, having the process take too long. ANA has a Procurement Task Force (more info here – http://www.ana.net/content/show/id/procurement-task-force) that helps procurement better understand marketing / advertising.

––––––

Agency Search Consultants

The speed at which technology is changing the advertising landscape is breathtaking. New advertising technologies that were once fresh can seem so yesterday in just a few months. This activity is not making running an advertising agency any easier as agencies have to keep their eyes on both today's and tomorrow's roads.

This era of complexity is no different for advertisers who are looking for agencies that can help them navigate the ever-changing marketing communications landscape. I believe that this onslaught of marketing options is driving the continued use of search consultants.

Today there are 26 search consultants listed on the 4A's website. There are many more when you add in local consultants. Search consultants act as personal shoppers for larger advertisers trying to locate the perfect agency out of hundreds, even thousands, of specific agency options. It is estimated that about 10% to 15% of all searches use the services of a consultant. I suspect that the number of consultant led pitches is well over 50% for clients that have large budgets, complicated accounts, and now, highly specialized agency searches.

The Yin And Yang Of Search Consultants.

First the Yin.

Advertising agencies have always had mixed feelings about search consultants as gatekeepers. LOL. How's that for an understatement.

On the positive side, search consultants help their clients select the best-suited agencies for review and manage the selection process so it's efficient for both parties. Most clients simply haven't had the experience in crafting and managing a well-designed agency search and don't have the time or expertise to examine all the agency options. Search consultant experience and expertise is beneficial to the advertising industry by reducing the number of wide-net agency RFP's and reviews that waste both client and agency time. The consultants help advertisers hone their agency search objectives, craft search guidelines, and navigate the wide sea of agency options.

Five key questions should start all searches.

1. **Does the agency have a significant competitive account conflict?**
   Many clients start their selection process by determining if the agency
   has a conflict. Conflicts range from logical direct conflicts (an agency
   can't have two breakfast cereal accounts), to corporate conflicts where
   an agency might not have a cereal account but has a chewing gum
   account whose parent company also manufacturers a cereal.

   In many cases, conflicts live solely in the mind of the client. One of
   my favorite advertising sayings is: having one competitive account
   is an insurmountable conflict, having more than one makes you a
   category expert.

2. **What are the agency's capabilities and specialties?** Search consultants, either through personal experience or their agency information
   database (more on this later), can help pinpoint agencies that have
   the capabilities that meet their client's marketing objectives. When I
   worked at a huge international agency, we offered a global footprint.
   At my own agency, we specialized in sports marketing. Consultants
   should efficiently help with this vetting process.

3. **Does the agency have the right talent and enough bandwidth?**
   Advertisers want to hit the ground running when they hire a new
   agency. The staff talent, skill-sets, experience, and capacity of an
   agency to meet the need for speed can be a critical selection decision.
   Consultants know agency depth, talent resources, and if the right
   agency might be too stretched in the short term by the process of
   onboarding a new account.

4. **Is the agency experienced in the client's category?** Again, given
   the speed of marketing (and possibly the short tenure of CMO's),
   clients look for agencies and agency staff that have experience in
   their categories. This can cut both ways as some clients look for

agencies that will come in with a fresh perspective and an ability to not do the same old, same old. However in most cases, prior experience rules because clients think that their category is complex and has a steep learning curve. I don't agree. But my perspective is beside the point.

5. **Will there be chemistry and love?** Given the fact that most agencies are experienced, professional, smart, creative, and strategic, selecting the right agency from a short-list often comes down to cultural fit. This element of match making isn't easy for you to control. It does however, point to your need to fully vet the clients that you will meet with. Even a simple Google or LinkedIn profile search can lead to personal or corporate insights that can be leveraged – or be the reason not to participate in a pitch.

Your matchmaking prowess will come into play when you select your agency team. Bringing an avowed atheist to the Vatican pitch might not be a perfect fit.

That's the Yin. Now for the Yang.

The biggest issue that advertising agencies have with search consultants is that some, and I stress some, consultants charge agencies for inclusion in their agency databases. This double dipping or "pay for play" is ripe for conflicts (what if the best agency for the client didn't pay up and isn't in the database?) and seems unethical. In my opinion, building an agency capabilities and information database should be the cost of doing business for search consultants.

Another issue, primarily for smaller agencies, is agency brand awareness. With so many large, mid-size, and small agencies, how can search consultants ever really know all of the best-fit agencies? The default will always be to go larger then mid-sized, and then, well, good luck smaller agencies.

Depending on who you talk to, there are over 4,000 marketing communications agencies in the USA. There is simply no way that consultants will know of every agency. If a search consultant is running a search for a specialist mobile agency how can that consultant really know of every suitable option? In this case, choosing a mid-sized agency with a mobile specialty might represent the most efficient solution even if it means excluding an agency run by the two best mobile developers in the business. Clearly, this needle in the haystack issue is shared by agencies themselves. In this case, it is incumbent for uber specialist agencies to figure out how to build their brand awareness with the right set of consultants.

Pitch Implications: You Got The Call

If a search consultant has contacted your agency, I suggest that you initially spend some time trying to understand their specific motivations and criteria related to the search. This will help you to be highly efficient in your responses. I think that it is important to follow these simple early-stage guidelines.

Say thank you. But, not too effusively.

Answer every question in order and in detail. This is your chance to begin to look sharp, professional and experienced. Helpful is a good thing. Remember, they are working for the client and not for you.

Find one way to quickly look strategic. This might be a savvy question seeking clarification of a client's objectives or the delivery of an early insight that might also help the consultant look sharp herself.

Don't be too pushy. Respect that the consultant is as time-stretched as you are.

Finally, some consultants have easily been in a lifetime of pitches. Their perspective after sitting through hundreds of hours of agency professionals trying to deliver their agency sales pitch is instructive. I asked a couple of the leading agency search consultants for their best and worst pitch moments. Some are illuminating, and some are laughable, unless of course, you recognize your own agency.

Two Search Consultants' Expert Opinions: Russel Wholwerth and Darren Woolley

Whether or not your agency will ever be included in a search run by an agency search consultant, experienced search experts can help us all better understand elements of the search process and how clients select agencies.

To get an expert opinion on how search consults work, I turned to two international experts. Russel Wholwerth is based in Los Angeles, and Darren Woolley is in Melbourne.

INTERVIEW
Russel Wholwerth, Owner, External View Consulting Group

Russel Wholwerth has been advising companies around the world on all aspects of marketing agency supplier management for 15 years. He is a serial entrepreneur who was an owner of Select Resources, a founding partner of Ark Advisors, and the founder of External View. All three have conducted thousands of national and international agency searches.

PL: What are the primary benefits that you offer your clients?

Russel: We provide intimate knowledge of a wide range of marketing resources. Beyond just knowing who the agencies are, we visit several hundred agencies a year, so we have a pretty in-depth knowledge of many agencies.

We have over 15 years' experience running agency searches, so we can advise on the most appropriate way to run a search. One size does not fit all. Therefore having this depth of experience and starting from a position of independence are major benefits.

PL: Since agency compensation is such a hot topic, can you tell me how agency search consultants are remunerated? Is there a standard fee?

Russel: I can't talk about how other consultants are compensated — and I would be careful not to generalize because I think there is a broad spectrum of methodologies. I will focus on how we determine our fees. We have fee ranges for searches, which are predicated on the anticipated number of man-hours it takes to complete the job. International searches take a lot longer to complete and often have significant travel requirements, and they are not priced the same as domestic searches.

I have heard that some consultants charge a back-end fee to the winning agency. We work for clients – not agencies – so we would not do this.

I also think you have to factor in the large number of consultants who charge agencies some type of fee. They charge clients less for searches since the agency fees are subsidizing the cost of the search.

PL: Do you have an optimal agency search system? Do you always do an RFI, then an RFP, and finally chemistry meetings that lead to the selection of a shortlist?

Russel: There are many different types of searches: you can't do the same process for a media search as you would a search for an events marketing agency.

We have an approach, but not a process. Each project is different, and we build the process to meet the unique needs of each client. You have to perform some level of diligence, and that can take many forms. Chemistry is a critically important part of sourcing professional services firms. To us, the question is what level of diligence needs to be done, and what is the metric by which the agencies will be judged? The more senior the client, the more creative our approach to the search.

PL: How long does the selection process usually take?

Russel: The typical domestic search takes about 12 weeks.

PL: What percentage of your searches now include procurement?

Russel: For us, about 75% of searches involve procurement. In some cases, we are hired directly by procurement. In other cases, they are an observer until we get into the RFP stage.

PL: How do you build your database of agencies? For example, you recently completed a pitch for the Panda Express account that was awarded to Omaha's Bailey Lauerman. How did you find an agency in Nebraska?

Russel: We have over 9,000 agencies in our database, and we subscribe to several other services that provide us with agency names. We ask that agencies register on our web site.

PL: I assume that you get a lot of incoming from agencies. How could a small to mid-sized agency get your attention? What attributes should they have before they bother making contact?

Russel: We get at least 20 to 30 inquiries from agencies every week. Most agencies act as if they have no clue how we operate or that they will need to really stand out to generate interest.

Great work will always get our attention. Also, agencies that are off the standard deviation curve excite us. Too many agencies sound and look alike.

PL: Are awards important to your clients? Bailey Laureman won Ad Age's 2013 national Small Agency of The Year. Is this type of industry recognition important to clients?

Russel: Awards are important in that they provide external third-party validation. However, not all awards are equal. Awards that measure effectiveness and creativity are more highly valued, as are international awards due to the level of competition. Many clients are reluctant to hire an agency they have never heard of, so this external validation is useful.

Furthermore, awards are a way for agencies to get on the map. We pride ourselves on being one step ahead of the formal recognition by being aware of these agencies before they are on the radar screen.

PL: Do your clients usually ask for spec creative? If so, how often does that work eventually get used?

Russel: The majority of clients desire spec creative. In some cases, when a company needs a new campaign, spec creative is justified. For most clients, spec creative is the metric that decides the winning agency.

We have observed over the last 15 years that the agency that wins a spec creative contest is not necessarily the agency for the long haul. In other words, spec creative is not necessarily a good measuring stick for determining the most appropriate agency. Spec creative sometimes get used, but most of it ends up on the cutting room floor.

PL: Many agencies tell me that they do not know what other agencies are in the pitch. What is the point of this cone of silence?

Russel: We usually try to keep the initial long list confidential for political reasons. For a popular brand search that gets in the press, it is not uncommon for us to receive inquiries from hundreds of agencies (of which most are appropriate). Publishing a long list of agencies in that case just gives these agencies another reason to demand to be included in the process, because so-and-so is in the pitch. We always disclose the agencies at some point in the process.

Agencies need to understand that most agency searches are not government tenders in which there is an obligation to the public to disclose all aspects of the process and all bidders. This is a private-sector procurement process, and there is absolutely no obligation to make any aspect of the pitch public.

Let me throw the question back at you. Why do agencies need to know who is in the pitch? Will they pitch differently? Will they pitch harder?

PL: I think that once the client selects the short list, they should share it with the finalist agencies. This information helps the agencies to do at least two things. First, it provides a way for the agencies to make one final determination if they should go through the grueling effort of

pitching the account. Second, this competitive intelligence might help the agencies to hone their point of view and ensure that they craft a unique, and competitive story. This should benefit the client.

Russel: We always disclose who will be in the finals as well as the role and title of each client attendee.

PL:Some agencies spend tens and even hundreds of thousands of dollars on pitches. Is this crazy, or is it what it takes to win?

Russel: Beyond organic growth, pitching is a way to grow an agency. The new business win rate is also a critical indicator of agency health and vitality.

I suppose an agency owner could be delusional and wait around for prospects to inquire if the agency would handle their account. Or, they could invest in a new business program. Agencies that do not win any new business are often dying agencies, so I think it is crazy not to invest in your future.

Good agency financial managers will realize there is an ROI associated with new business, and they will decide what the appropriate level of investment should be to increase agency billings by $X million.

PL: I'd imagine that by the time you get to a short list, any one of the agencies could do great work for the client. What have been the presentation factors that have helped you make the final decision?

Russel: In many cases, it comes down to proving that they are good listeners who are focused on the client's key issues and requirements. Agencies should concentrate on demonstrating their understanding of the client's business, and category, and come to the presentation with great ideas.

PL: Conversely, are there any standard presentation blunders that agencies make – over and over?

Russel: Agencies can often appear tone-deaf to the client's needs. These agencies tend to be intoxicated with their own attributes like the number of offices they have around the world.

PL: What makes a great leave behind? Does having an expensive 'creative' leave behind make a difference?

Russel: The leave behind should be a record of the presentation and provide information that the client can refer to in their deliberations. I am not a fan of crazy boxes. Many leave behinds today are digital and use custom landing pages and simple USB drives.

PL: Final question. You've mentioned that many pitches use an antiquated approach based on the world of 1980's TV advertising. Given today's complex media and multi-platform marketing environment, what decision-making metrics and values should clients be looking for?

Russel: Media today is much more complex than in the TV days, and agencies should look like collaborators who can work in teams. They should look like they can move on a dime and be able to discuss how they create fast-paced social media programs. Case histories are especially important here.

————

INTERVIEW
Darren Woolley, Founder and Managing Director, TrinityP3

TrinityP3 is an independent strategic marketing management consultancy based in Melbourne, Australia. It works across continents and has 40 of Australia's top 100 advertisers using its services. The company assists marketers, advertisers, and procurement with agency search & selection, agency engagement & alignment, and agency monitoring & benchmarking to ensure maximum performance in efficiency and effectiveness of their advertising and marketing budgets.

Darren started as a scientist, got into advertising as a copywriter, and ended up a creative director. After 15 years in advertising, he realized when marketers and their agencies work well together, amazing things happen. He established TrinityP3 in 2000 as an independent marketing management consulting company that provides marketers and advertisers with benchmarks, training, and advice on how to maximize the value of their marketing budgets.

PL: What are the primary benefits that you offer your clients?

Darren: We provide intimate industry knowledge, independent advice, and proven methodology in assisting marketers and advertisers to select, manage, and remunerate their full roster of agencies to maximize the value of the budget.

PL: Since agency compensation is such a hot topic, can you tell me how agency search consultants are remunerated? Is there a standard fee?

Darren: We charge a fixed fee to the advertiser for the particular service they require. This is a fixed fee and not reconciled against head count hours, but instead a successful outcome. Unlike some consultants, we do not charge fees to agencies. We do not charge success fees or sign up fees or any fees at all to any agency.

We also guarantee the outcome, by offering to rerun the pitch if the selected agency relationship does not last 12 months. In 14 years, we have only had to do this once.

PL: Do you have an optimal agency search system? Do you always do an RFI, RFP, and chemistry meetings that lead to the selection of a shortlist?

Darren: We offer a range of methodologies in running a pitch, from our "pitch in a day" process to a fully managed "tender process". There is not one process to suit all. Instead, we work with the advertiser and procurement to customize the process to deliver the successful outcome required.

It means we can work with all processes with experience and expertise in every process type.

PL: How long does the selection process usually last?

Darren: The process can be as short as six weeks for the "pitch in a day" process or up to 5 months for a multi-country, multi-disciplined tender process. The length of the process will depend on the scope and require-ment of the specific project. The important thing in regards to time is to develop and agree a timeline up front, and make sure all stakeholders, including the participating agencies, are informed of this timeline at each stage of the process.

PL: What percentage of your searches now include procurement?

Darren: About two thirds of searches now include procurement.

PL: How do you build your database of agencies?

Darren: We have an online database on our website. Here agencies can create their own login and profile, which is free and totally secure. The TrinityP3 agency register has profiles of a full range of agency types from media to social to digital to public relations and sales promotion and more from across the APAC region and beyond. Agencies from anywhere in the world have the ability to register here, and there are more than 12,000 agencies, of the various types, currently registered with us. We use this register to stay up-to-date across the industry players.

PL: I assume that you get a lot of incoming from agencies. How could a small to mid-sized agency get your attention? What attributes should they have before they bother making contact?

Darren: Interestingly, we have noted a change in the marketing mix. Even advertisers from multinational companies with a global or regional agency alignment are increasingly interested in small to mid-size agencies to improve and often compensate for deficiencies in the aligned agency.

Therefore mid-sized agencies with particular strengths are increasingly important and in demand in the agency mix. As are smaller agencies that can articulate and prove a core specialist competency which makes them distinctive from others. This is a real benefit.

PL: Are awards important to your clients? Do they help them make decisions about the subjective nature of advertising?

Darren: The short answer is awards are generally not important to clients. Certainly there are a few of our clients that would select an agency based solely on awards won. Effectiveness awards have some credibility, but the winning of awards is more about substantiating other attributes of the agency than being a differentiator in its own right.

PL: Do your clients usually ask for spec creative? If so, how often does that work eventually get used?

Darren: We recommend that an advertiser never ask for speculative creative. In less than 10% of pitches we will ask for creative, but our preferred model is to use strategic workshops between the advertiser and the agency as a way of determining the agencies capabilities, chemistry, collaboration, and creativity. Where speculative work is asked for, it is usually to visualize the strategic solution developed in the workshops so that it can be shared with other internal stakeholders who did not participate in the workshop, such as the CEO or even the board.

PL: Many agencies tell me that they do not know what other agencies are in the pitch. What is the point of this cone of silence?

Darren: We do not release the list of agencies for a number of reasons. First, because the agencies sign a non-disclosure agreement, and we believe this applies both ways, so we should only release the names of the participating agencies with their permission. Second, we have had situations where the list was released, and agencies have felt it more important to compete against the other agencies rather than focus on solving the advertiser's requirement of selecting the best agency. This has included spreading rumors about their competitors in the process to directly making allegations against other agencies.

PL: They also tell me that they often don't know what individual clients will be in the final presentation. What is the reason for anonymity?

Darren: We always inform the agency of who will be attending from the client for the chemistry meetings, workshops, and presentations. Likewise we ask the agencies to provide the same information on who is attending from the agency. We believe this secrecy is counterproductive and not conducive to creating an open and fair selection process or establishing a productive and sustainable advertiser / agency relationship.

PL: Some agencies spend tens and even hundreds of thousands of dollars on pitches. Is this crazy, or is it what it takes to win?

Darren: It is crazy investing hundreds of thousands of dollars on a pitch if the account is worth only a hundred thousand dollars. This is a business decision, and agencies must make the decision on whether to pitch or not and how much to invest in the pitch based on their best assessment of the value and the chance of winning the business. If this is a multi-million dollar piece of business, then investing a hundred thousand dollars to increase your chance of winning the business could be a good investment. But to be honest, if the process is run correctly, then usually this is not required to select the best agency.

PL: I'd imagine that by the time you get to a short list, any one of the agencies could do great work for the client. What have been the presentation factors that have helped you make the final decision?

Darren: Again, we avoid speculative creative work as it is a poor criteria for selecting an agency and leaves more questions than it answers, such as: "They may have fluked the solution here, what is the process that led to it and is it reproducible?" or "Who actually did the work, and will they be working on my business?"

One of our success factors is that the advertisers find it hard to make a decision because all of the agencies were excellent. This means we have made a good selection and recommendation.

But interestingly, what wins pitches is often the least manageable of all – human chemistry. Do these people share our values? Can we work productively together? Do we trust each other? Beyond capabilities, experience and expertise, this is the deciding factor.

PL: Conversely, are there any standard presentation blunders that agencies make – over and over?

Darren: Agencies make many blunders, and we have shared many of these on the TrinityP3 blog as a way to inform and teach agencies on how to avoid these.

The biggest and most common, and it goes directly to chemistry, is spending all your time talking about yourself and not engaging the advertiser in discussion or conversation, or not listening to what they are saying because you are too absorbed in yourself. Believe me this still happens more often than you think.

PL: What makes a great leave behind? Does having an expensive 'creative' leave behind make a difference?

Darren: Clarity, relevance, and interest. Make it clear. Make it relevant. And create interest in what you have to say using all you have at your disposal as a communications professional.

Too many agencies waffle. Make the layout and copy difficult to read. Use design to make it look 'creative' but are difficult to read. Or the agencies spend a fortune dressing it up.

A mud pie with frosted icing on top may look nice, but it is still a mud pie.

PL: Any other thoughts that can help agencies better mange their pitch processes to win more pitches?

Darren: My advice to all agencies is "pitch less and win more". Do not participate in a pitch just because the opportunity is provided to you. Assess that opportunity to determine if it is right for you.

This means when you are offered a pitch opportunity, take the time to interrogate the opportunity with questions about process, size of project or contract, and expectations. If you do not get the answers you want, then do not pitch.

Next look at your existing clients. Do you have the time and resources to participate in the pitch without a negative impact on the current clients? Finally, if you are successful, is this the type of advertiser you would want as a client? Because if you answer no to any of these questions then you are better off withdrawing respectfully as another opportunity will come your way.

———

Procurement. The P-Word.

Few words strike more fear and loathing in the hearts of agency management than "procurement". This P-Word gets its rap from being viewed as an impediment to an advertising agency's ability to sell its strategic and creative expertise vs. having to sell on price. The role of procurement isn't that simple. And this is another Yin and Yang.

Agencies often view procurement as the bad guy. Procurement executives are perceived as the group at the client that initiates reviews based on a timetable that disregards current agency success (take that incumbents), has no clue about the wonderful world of marketing magic that advertising agencies deliver, views agencies as being interchangeable, and worse, that it's all just a numbers game. What agency would ever want to negotiate with procurement? The low bid wins the account. Price over art. It kills the soul.

I think that this is a bad rap. Sometimes.

I say sometimes because I think that we can divide procurement executives into two groups. The first, my Yin, work at larger clients and have a few years experience working with marketing services agencies. This experienced procurement executive understands the complexities of the client agency relationship and marketing itself. In many cases, they have been schooled by organizations like the ANA to better understand how marketing works, its bottom line value, and how agency relationships are born and managed for success. These relationships span the strategic and creative deliverable, usually the prevue of CMO's, to financials, operations, compensation, and contracts which are the expertise of procurement.

The good news is that procurement executives, contrary to the popular belief held by creative directors, actually have a left and right side of the brain. Here is a revealing quote from Craig Brown when he was Intel's VP Materials Procurement & Supply Chain (from the 2010 AdAge article, "Procurement: We're About Value, Not Price"). I believe that it is important to note that according to Craig, procurement execs were well aware of the relationship of big ideas to sales *way back* in 2010.

> *"You want to get the A-team on your account because the creativity often comes from that 5% to 10% of the agency's population that has the whizzy brain idea. So you want to be careful you're not just paying for warm bodies, that you actually have an alignment of the quality and creativity. That was a wake-up call to me. I didn't see it as extensive with some of our other contracts as I did in the agency world."*

My Yang.

The second group of procurement decision makers are, in fact, clueless when it comes to judging agencies. They are corporate purchase decision makers that have been put into the agency selection process without much, if any, idea of how marketing works. They are inexperienced in working with agencies and in understanding the complexities of marketing. They live up to our greatest fear that the procurement department is going to apply the same performance metrics to the art of a service like advertising that they apply to buying office supplies. While this might be an overstatement, in many cases it is unfortunately very close to the truth.

So I am agreeing with some agency executives that procurement can be the boogey man.

Pitch Implications

I am not sure what agencies can do to alleviate the problem of an inexperienced procurement executive other than to go with the flow and make sure that agency management works to try to understand the client's motivations. It is important to recognize that all procurement executives are far from evil. They have an important corporate role to play and come with a financially oriented perspective. They report to the COO or CFO, not the CMO. The smartest agencies understand this and work within the constraints.

I think that it is imperative to consider the following mind-set when negotiating with procurement.

Purchasing goods and services at the right price is integral to a corporation's bottom line management and efficiency.

A well-designed procurement system will help manage costs while increasing innovation. As an experienced third-party, procurement can help the client's marketing group focus business building objectives.

Procurement executives often view marketing as an unwieldy and difficult to judge cost center. Note to agencies: it is. The value of creative services isn't as easy to determine as purchasing IT services. Let's face it… it can be difficult to prove the true value of ideas. Gerry Preece (see the following interview) confirms this and goes further to highlight that CMO's themselves are often flummoxed when they need to justify agency and marketing expenses. Determining the ROI of marketing is often the most stressful part of a CMO's job.

I believe that the way to build trust with procurement is to talk their language. The best marketing and advertising does, in fact, deliver a positive ROI. I am sure that agencies that are willing to discuss success metrics, can point to the use of quantitative measurement and marketing analytics, will be talking the same language as procurement. As is the case with all great marketing and sales, understanding the target market (in this case the Chief Procurement Officer) is essential to building trust and ultimately selling a profitable service.

Here's an idea that will foster a sense of alignment between the agency and procurement.

I suggest that agencies mention their own attention to financial detail in RFP's and in the pitch, even if the client isn't asking about it. Sound like you really understand the financial issues and ISO 9000 quality management associated with procurement. Consider having an evergreen white paper on the importance of financial management that you send ahead of your pitch.

Work on winning procurement over. Don't just bitch about them.

INTERVIEW
Gerry Preece, Owner, Preece Consulting

When I wanted to get the perspective of a procurement expert, I went directly to Gerry Preece the ex-head of marketing procurement for Proctor & Gamble, the world's largest advertiser. He is the author, along with Russel Wholwerth, of 2013's *Buying Less For Less. How to Avoid the Marketing Procurement Dilemma*, the definitive book on how advertising agencies should work with procurement. Gerry and Russel also led a 4A's series of national seminars on how agencies can work more effectively with client procurement organizations.

I think that you will find Gerry's perspective both enlightening and an opportunity to help you craft your message to win over any procurement executives in the decision making process. While you are at it, you might want to brush up on your agency's negotiation skills. You'll see what I mean.

PL: Most advertising agencies do not understand the role of procurement in agency selection. Can you help us out?

Gerry: Not only do ad agencies misunderstand the role of procurement, marketers themselves often don't think about the role clearly either.

In my opinion, Procurement should play the role of strategic sourcing professionals that includes:

Methodical development of internal needs and wants
Methodical revaluation of external capabilities
Connecting the two in smart, strategic ways
Contingency planning
Relationship management
Not making marketing decisions
Work in conjunction with marketing leaders
Ongoing work, not episodic
Lead the work of accountability

Procurement should hold advertising clients accountable for creating clear expectations and deliverables, while holding the agencies accountable for performance, efficiency, and procedures (where appropriate).

Not everyone sees it that way. Some think Procurement should look for ways to cut costs. Some of these people are CEOs, CPOs, CFOs, and even CMOs – sometimes.

Agencies need to know that not all Procurement organizations will fit the above, and they need to avoid treating Procurement as 'monochromatic' or 'monolithic' across all organizations.

PL: You were the Global Director of Marketing Procurement at P&G. How was your approach different than your colleagues who procured standard materials?

Gerry: There are ten ways in which Marketing is structurally, fundamentally, intrinsically different than every other spend pool handled by Procurement (which include: materials, chemicals, packaging, production services, health care, food service, facilities management, travel services, manufactured items, etc.). The book Russel Wholwerth and I wrote (*Buying Less for Less*) details these ten areas at length. Because of the fundamental differences between Marketing and other client purchases, the approach has to be different.

Four key ways in which my approach was different, "The Four Right Things":

1. Use the right metrics (not "savings").

2. The right metric is "Value Add".

3. Mange savings year-on-year.

4. Manage cost avoidance (money not spent that would otherwise have been spent). These include incremental profit resulting from better campaigns, better marketing, better agencies, increased sales, and the associated incremental profit, etc. Remember when estimating incremental profit that fixed costs are already covered.

When the above is applied, people will naturally gravitate to the Incremental Profit area, as that is the big lever. Nobody else in Procurement used this metric – and I had to fight that.

Procurement executives should have:

The right mindset: I viewed my job as adding value, not just cost cutting.

The right skills: Marketing Procurement people need to be good strategic sourcers. Plus, they should have broad business skills (e.g. the discussion above about incremental profit and metrics should be second nature) and good relational skills – because process rigor, which exists elsewhere, doesn't fit in marketing. So you have to succeed by working with others – others who don't have to work with you.

The right assignment: All the above takes time – so these are longer-term assignments and should last for several years. Credibility, knowledge of marketing's complexity, and relationships are critical and take time.

PL: Was P&G's procurement department involved in every agency selection? Are there types of searches where procurement should not play a role?

Gerry: Provided Procurement plays the right role (strategic sourcing experts) and applies the "Four Right Things" (outlined earlier), they should be involved in ALL agency searches and selections. Conversely, if they do not meet those criteria, then in my opinion, they have no business in *any* agency decision.

Procurement at P&G today is involved in every decision. It was during my years as well, limited only by Procurement department capacity. Also, "involvement" has migrated over the last fifteen years at P&G from "involved in an advisory capacity" to "key decision maker". At the same time, Procurement "owned" sourcing for promotional marketing services (coupons, direct mail, etc.) and eventually took on more ownership for the more strategic stuff, like media and creative agency selection.

PL: Agencies think that the primary roll of procurement is to cut costs and reduce spending. They think that procurement does not understand or appreciate the 'magic' of advertising. Is this true?

Gerry: Sadly, in too many cases, yes. But in many cases, Procurement is doing a pretty good job – there's a bell curve.

However, when things are not good, agencies terribly misdiagnose the problem. What they fail to recognize is that in these cases, Procurement individuals are not making up the rules regarding the role of Procurement. They have been sent by someone above them to do exactly what they're doing. Somebody – perhaps a CPO or CFO or CMO – has given them the cost savings remit and deliverable and they are the problem. The Procurement practitioner is doing what they are being measured on. Attack the scorecard (the metrics) and the person who issues the scorecard – otherwise agencies will waste their time, and nothing will improve.

Again, there is not one homogeneous definition of a "Procurement" department. Instead there are hundreds of them, and they are all different in terms of metrics, deliverables, areas of focus, emphasis on savings, etc. Agencies need to stop complaining, and get smart.

Figure out what Procurement's role is for a given client – and figure it out fast.

If it's wrong (not the "Four Right Things"), then effectively influence the changes needed (see *Buying Less for Less*), and this usually starts by engaging the CMO.

Stop acting powerless and drive the changes: agencies have a lot of power and a lot at stake but incorrectly think they are impotent. They simply need to see the problem clearly ("Four Right Things"), and attack the problem smartly (articulate the ten differences and "Four Right Things" to the CMO).

PL: You've mentioned the idea that marketing is an investment not a one-time purchase. Can you elaborate?

Gerry: Unlike every other spend area that Procurement touches, we spend dollars on marketing because we *want* to, not because we *have* to. And we *want* to spend marketing dollars because we get a return on those dollars. (If not, stop spending!) And therefore, any discussion of "savings" is silly and irrelevant. It only changes the denominator. Why would we not also, at the same time, look at changing the numerator (return)? Surely when we fiddle with one, we impact the other, right? So the idea becomes to look at ROI, not at just the spend alone.

PL: How can procurement help CMO's measure results and metrics?

Gerry: Procurement can only help here by applying unbiased and objective operational rigor. We can make no judgments about the quality of the marketing.

But Procurement can and should collect the info, apply it to a system of metrics, and use that as one of many criteria to make decisions. This is similar to what Procurement does elsewhere – we don't decide on food service quality or performance; food service pros do. We don't decide on a chemical's performance or manufacturing handle-ability; manufacturing pros do. What Procurement does is rigorously and objectively collect the data and bring it to bear on sourcing decisions.

PL: We all know that CMO tenure can be an issue. How does this factor into how procurement works with CMO's in agency selection?

Gerry: Generally, Procurement serves the CMO, so our role will change depending on the CMO. I'm not aware of any situations where Procurement selects agencies and the CMO gets "stuck" with those decisions.

Procurement has an obligation to sort out reasoned rationale from favoritism. If a new CMO wants to fire the old agency and hire his "favorite" agency simply because he's pals with them, Procurement has an obligation to push back and to insist on a fair and objective process. But, in every case I can think of, CMO's (not Procurement) ultimately make that call.

PL: When it comes to contracts and service agreements, are agencies good negotiators? If not, how can they learn this art?

Gerry: In 95% of the cases, agencies are babes being led to slaughter. Terrible. Naive. Wishful. They get creamed. They are up against professional negotiators, and they often put their unskilled (in negotiations), nicest, most accommodating people against Procurement. It's generally a blood bath.

The biggest problem (my opinion) is the ridiculous love affair out there with "principle based" negotiation approaches (i.e. *Getting to Yes*). These are win-win approaches we've all fallen in love with because we hate conflict, we hate negotiating with mean people, and we want to live in harmony.

The key problem with all that is that Procurement people are schooled in "positional" negotiating strategies and tactics (win-lose), and positional beats principled every time.

The second biggest problem is that many agencies don't do any formal negotiation training for their folks. They should be training in negotiations skills and develop strong negotiators. And, they should embrace positional negotiations skills – because that's often how Procurement's playing the game.

PL: How can agencies demonstrate their understanding of the role of procurement when they are pitching?

Gerry: Ask what the role is and demonstrate you know there is no "one way" Marketing Procurement folks operate.

Ask what their metrics are – cost savings? Value-add? If value-add, how is that measured?

Ask who the Procurement executive reports to and ask what they are being held accountable to deliver.

Lay out a simple strategic sourcing model and ask them to explain their role in that perspective.

Get great back office hygiene, and make it a deliberate part of your capabilities presentation. Include it in your video credentials and deck. Proactively address it with statements like (I'm making this up): "We practice ISO 9000 rigor in our accounts payable and receivables area; we strategically source all our third party services with professional buyers who know their markets and actively negotiate competitive rates on post-production work, equipment rental, etc.; we review our vendor's procedures and challenge them on off-shoring where it makes sense; we periodically audit our vendors, etc." Don't wait for Procurement to ask about these things.

Proactively manage the message, which is that "we spend every dime thoughtfully, carefully, and professionally – and we run a tight ship when it comes to financial matters and third party arrangements."

Negotiation

Negotiation is another word that strikes fear into agency executives. In my agency career, I didn't find many agency leaders that looked forward to negotiating their client service contracts with a well-positioned client. We better get over this. Why? I want to go back to Gerry Preece's comment about agency negotiation skills:

"In 95% of the cases, agencies are babes being led to slaughter. Terrible. Naive. Wishful. They get creamed. They are up against professional negotiators, and they often put their unskilled (in negotiations), nicest, most accommodating people against Procurement. It's generally a blood bath."

Hearing that 95% of P&G agencies are like *"babes being led to slaughter"* is a very painful point to digest. Note that, in P&G's case, we are talking about some serious big time agencies.

I can understand that going up against a well-schooled Procurement executive might seem a seriously tough job given their senior corporate role and expertise. But, I have also had a very difficult time negotiating with a local Honda dealer client. Simply put, in my experience, clients are much better negotiators than agency managers. It could be that we want the deal way too badly for our own sake.

It is baffling to me that I never took a course in negotiation. Why I didn't try to learn how to negotiate is crazy given the agency industry's need to wrestle every percentage point of margin out of our deals. The only thing that makes me feel better about this deficiency is that I am clearly not alone.

After interviewing Gerry, I had to find a negotiation expert to help me begin to understand how to help all of us become better negotiators. Marty Finkle's recommendations are both insightful, and unfortunately, occasionally all too obvious.

INTERVIEW
Marty Finkle, Scotwork NA, CEO

Marty Finkle is a negotiation industry expert and sought-after speaker. He leads the team of Scotwork NA negotiators, who work with more than 100 companies in a range of industries. Scotwork's client list includes network and medium size marketing communications agencies and major corporations including Boeing, Google, and Michelin. Through his work on negotiation strategy, process, and behaviors, many organizations have achieved an exceptional return on investment, while participants have been able to adapt their new negotiation skills to other workplace and personal situations.

PL: Here's a revealing quote on agency negotiation from an earlier interview I did with Gerry Preece who was the head of procurement at Proctor & Gamble. "In 95% of cases, agencies are like babes being led to slaughter – terrible, naïve, wishful. They get creamed." Is that your experience in your dealings with advertising agencies? Are they lambs to the slaughter?

Marty: I think a lot of times what happens is that agencies go into these meetings thinking they're terribly weak, and part of the reason is they do believe the other side has all the power – especially if it's procurement. That makes them very sheep-ish. It's not right or wrong, it's just the way agencies have been trained over the years. Something I've said to a number of ad execs is: we train our buyers how to treat us, and we've done it for years, but we don't train them how to treat us differently.

So as they go in, they're really sheep-ish, and then they let the buyer take the reigns and really take control of the meeting. Here's the word: they *are* like lambs going into the slaughter, because they're at the whim of whatever the buyer's looking to do.

PL: Do you think that agencies are even walking in with a good understanding of what their goals are for the meeting, or are they just looking for the other party to state what the objectives are?

Marty: I think agencies are walking in with what they would like to get, but I don't think they plan out what they actually intend to get out of the meeting. I think they let the meeting just roll. Now in a discovery meeting, of course you're going to do that, because there's a place for discovery, and it's for dialogue. But when they go into a negotiation meeting unprepared, of course the buyer's going to be in much more control.

When we work with agencies, one of the things that we always recommend to them to do is prepare the major issues they want to talk about, so that if the buyer pulls them off tune, if you will, they can go back at the list of their main issues they want to talk about, and focus on it. If the issue is the length of time it's going to take to deliver the project, or the amount of people that are going to be involved, or the rate card, we want them to get very serious about what their intentions are and what their limits are which they're willing to negotiate. If they understand these things before walking into negotiation, they're going be much more powerful in the dialogue, because when they get down the creative path, or the pricing path, they're going to be much more focused on what they really need out of the negotiation.

Don't wing it.

PL: Don't wing it seems obvious, but I know that agencies do just that. Do you coach your clients to practice negotiation before they walk into a room?

Marty: We do. We actually work with our agency clients on the whole preparation for an upcoming event. I'm thinking of a client we just did this with where they were the weaker party, or they perceived they were weaker than their customer. The agency customer was a huge brand - you'd know it. We had the agency prepare the issues they wanted to cover, the intentions of each one of the issues, what their limits were on the ones that had limits. If they got pushed on one of the areas, what were the things that they were going to trade for for every move they made. And then, what is the agency going to ask for in return if they do trade? And then, think through their negotiation positioning statement: how are they going to open and focus?

The other thing that we do Peter, that really makes the agency more powerful, is have them prepare as if they were the other side. So it's really important that they do prepare, and we do help them. We coach them and then allow them to actually hold the dialogue as if they were doing the negotiation with their particular client.

PL: And is there a right number or an optimum number of agency people that should be going into these negotiation sessions?

Marty: The coaching we give to our agencies is this: you need to establish a lead negotiator, the person who's going to actually run the negotiation – it's not always the CEO. It may the account manager, and in some cases, it may be the CFO if it's the contracting part of the negotiation.

But we always recommend that there's a leader there and what we call a summarizer. The leader actually runs the negotiation. The summarizer is the person who listens for all the nuances. If the leader misses something, the summarizer is there to pick it up and say "Hey, hold on one second 'Peter', what I just heard them tell you was they're willing to give us our price as long as we are willing to deliver the job in six weeks or less." In this case, the leader may not have heard that concession, but the summarizer did in his secondary role.

PL: Is there anything you can do to help agencies understand what the true motivation of a procurement negotiator is? For example, what *is* his job function? How does he receive his bonus?

Marty: A procurement person, first of all, is there to get you to give up things. The things may be your rates; it may be terms; it may be throwing in freebies. You've already made your agreement with the marketer, but procurement is there to then squeeze you on price. Their metric may be on price; their metric may also be on other values. So the thing that we tell our agencies and our ad execs, whether they're traditional ad, or digital, or PR, is ask the procurement person: How are you measured? What is a win for you?

I asked some procurement people the other day (I was speaking at a conference to a smaller group of 18 in the room before a large conference began), and I said okay you push agencies to give you for example, a 20% discount. They're all shaking their heads yes with big smiles on their faces. And I turned to each one of them and I said "What does 20% mean to you?" The first person says "2.3%". The next one says "6.8%". Nobody, *no one* even close to 20%. It was always south of it. I ask "so why do you ask for the 20?" They told me "Because agencies just give in and give us the 20." My metric is not 20 though. The point here is to probe the basis of the request and don't just give in on the % they are seeking. Find out the rationale and whatever small percentage you may give in, either take something away or trade for more of something including volume, other contractual parts, and other brand exposure. Don't just give in because it sets precedence.

PL: So do you think agencies, in the world of business, are by nature worse negotiators than other types of businesses?

Marty: I won't say worse negotiators. I think that part of what makes an agency tick is the CLIO and the excitement about the portfolio, the excitement about the ad, whether it's digital or hardcopy or whatever it is – the excitement. And what makes them weaker sometimes is how excited they are around the creative. It's not right or wrong, it just is.

So are agencies weaker? No, I think what they do is they get caught up in the excitement of the world that they live in and what they're trying to do in it. So if you get your CFO in the room, they may be harder on price than if you have a creative director in there. The creative director, occasionally the CEO, whoever has not been in this type of negotiation meeting in the past, tends to give things away quicker than anybody else. We teach creative directors that if they give something away they need to get something in return. That can go against an agency's grain sometimes, because they figure: I have to give in in order to win the deal, or the business, or the pitch.

PL: Are there a couple of tips that you could give either an owner or CEO of an agency? For example, what are two things that every agency manager should be thinking about when he's going in to negotiate with a client?

Marty: The first thing that's critical, if you're the CEO or you're the owner of the agency, and you're going in to negotiate with a client in a situation where somebody else has started the negotiation, is align your message. It's critical. So for example, if the account manager has gone into the negotiation, and the client says, "we want your CEO to come in to finalize the deal", we always recommend to the CEO that he allows the account manager to continue to lead the negotiation. The CEO is there as a summarizer. If you are in a situation where you need to give in, you turn to the account manager because you've planned it, then the account manager gives in, not the CEO. The reason we do it that way is because if the CEO is the one that gives something away, you must imagine that the client (whether the marketer or the procurement person), is going to skip the account manager in the future, and they will go directly to the CEO. That's not what the CEO wants.

The second is to prepare well and prepare as a team. If you can understand what you want out of the negotiation going into it, then you are more likely to come out getting the things you want. If you prepare well, it will help you propose your solutions first. You can gain power in your negotiation if you are the one out of the gate with the first proposal. If you prepare well, then you will be confident in your proposed solution.

As a bonus tip, make sure to prepare the team who will be there and then the others who may get called after the meeting to chip away at your organization. Get the CEO, CFO, Creative team or anyone who touches the negotiation on the same page with the same information based on your preparation so they don't inadvertently give something away that you did not intend to trade.

———

Agency Compensation

A Big Budget Question

You've decided to pitch for a large account or individual project. You've done your homework and assessed your chances. That's good.

But... will you eventually get paid enough to make this effort worthwhile? Will this be a profitable account when you factor in your RFI, RFP, and pitch costs? How long will it take to recoup all of these costs? If your profit margin is in the 20% range (high for most agencies), in an average pitch you might have to generate upwards of $100,000 in revenues on this new account just to recoup break-even expenses. Allow me to repeat myself: break even.

If this is an AOR client with some longer-term retention potential, you will be in a better position. If it's a project, you should be thinking very hard about how to manage down the costs of this pitch especially if it going to take you 90 to 120 days to get your first invoice paid. I have seen agencies go under because of new client start up expenses and delayed payments.

Here's another wrench to toss into the pitch machine. Do you know the client's compensation plan before you begin to pitch for their business?

While there is no one-size-fits-all type of client, my bet is that the client has had you go thorough the preliminary RFI / RFP process without a clear discussion of compensation. Somehow, you guessed at the ultimate value of this client and hoped that you would get clarification before the final pitch. My experience is that although an experienced client may have provided a general budget range, many clients don't get to a serious compensation discussion and negotiation until after you have pitched. I've read too many industry articles about agencies that have won pitches only to exit the relationship after they couldn't come to terms with the new client.

I asked Michael Jeary, President of Laughlin-Constable NY, about his experience in trying to get prospective clients to discuss their budgets ahead of pitching.

> *"I ask the 'What's your budget' kind of question whenever we are approached and initially briefed by a prospective client or search consultant on a new opportunity. It is exceedingly rare that I receive a response...more so when asked of a prospective client. Search consultants generally are more forthcoming, knowing why that piece of information is important to disclose upfront.... on so many fronts.*
>
> *I always had the impression that the spending or budget information was kept close to the vest by prospective clients because they thought that agencies typically create a response that's 'priced to budget' rather than 'priced to task'. Perhaps our industry deserves that lack of trust after so many years of doing just that."*

I think that we have all had similar experiences. I can see that in many cases, clients would like their agency to help them establish the budget based on their marketing objectives. Even in the best case scenario as described in the "ANA/4A's Guidelines For Agency Search" report, advertisers should at least provide a budget range in RFP's:

> *"Include a discussion on agency compensation early on. Don't provide a specific budget for agency compensation, but consider providing a budget range. Cost must fit for both parties. What the client is willing to pay must fit the economics of what the agency is able and willing to provide – at a profit."*

Clearly, even in a good situation, pitching is a crapshoot. Adding in not knowing how or how much you will get paid can lead to a disaster.

The Compensation Landscape

My Compensation "Wish List"…

Over the past ten years, the compensation screws have been tightened – hard. Maybe a bit too hard. Nothing like a global recession to drive agency profits down. That said, in order to begin to make what you deserve, you have to go into the pitch process, and ultimately, compensation negotiations with a very solid idea of how you want to get paid for your talent, ideas, and production.

Here is my wish list. I think that this scenario could form the basis of an interesting compensation discussion. It is based on recognizing the value of big ideas and ROI.

Critical note: I admit it's a *wish list*, but I am an optimist so why not start with a sweet objective.

In my "best of all possible world's" scenario, you will be paid using a three-part scale. This scale recognizes that you should be paid for big ideas at a higher rate than production services. After all, should you be charging the same rate for a HUGE business-building idea that you charge for production management?

1. The Big Idea. Get paid the big bucks for generating a Big Business Building Idea (BBBI). This is why the agency pays its most creative employees the bigger bucks, and shouldn't the client be paying you on the same scale? Did Allstate pay Leo Burnett a blended rate for the "Mayhem" TV campaign? What did Kia pay for those dancing hamsters?

Creating a system to get paid for a BBBI will not be easy. However, many clients are becoming interested in compensating their agencies for big business building ideas, and we now have a range of analytical tools that can help us relate the true value of ideas to brand success metrics. Importantly, even having this discussion can help you position your agency as one that understands the client's business objectives.

2. BBBI Management. This is the where the agency plans how to run with the big idea. In some cases, how and where you run the BBBI is a very creative process. Account, media, and digital planning require some serious grey matter to deal with the complexities of today's social media, mobile as well as digital, and traditional media choices and opportunities. You should be paid handsomely for planning how to run with the big creative idea.

3. BBBI execution. Execution includes production, media buying, programming, and any other service needed to execute the BBBI. Execution costs less. It can even be outsourced. Here is a real-world social media example of BBBI vs. the execution of BBBI. How much did Oreo's agency get paid for the big idea of the 2013 Super Bowl blackout tweet vs. the fee paid to write 140 characters and then hit send?

I think that this three-part scenario serves both the client and agency. It recognizes what the agency is actually hired to do – create business building marketing. It removes the problem of delivering a very big BBBI while being paid only for hours worked.

How do we get there?

Clients need to be very clear about what they expect the agency's work to accomplish. I always asked prospective clients about what would make them smile at the end of a campaign. Some clients could express their goals in quantitative terms like sales or market share gains (surprisingly, my Nike client couldn't) and some had more generalized goals. My favorite insight, generally from existing clients, is getting a perspective on their own personal performance metrics. Tying the agency's goals to the clients' personal goals makes a great deal of sense. I love that level of clarification. Regardless, if you can quantify the client's idea of success, then you can begin to figure out the value of that BBBI.

OK, Back To Reality

As is the case in any business relationship, the best partnerships are based on both parties thinking that what they are paying and being paid is fair. I can tell you that as someone who entered the advertising industry at the end of the Mad Men era, the 15% media commission compensation system often over paid agencies. I can also tell you as an agency CEO confronted with cost-plus or fixed fee based compensation in the age of ballooning media alternatives, we were occasionally underpaid.

This shift to lower margins has been exacerbated by new pressures being placed on marketing budgets: loss of CMO power, the ROI issue, the increasing role of procurement departments, and a sense at some clients that agencies are, by some freak of nature, way overpaid.

On the agency side, our labor and other overhead costs have not decreased. Marketing budgets are now spread across an increasing list of media options that have to be planned and managed, and there are increasingly more short-term projects vs. AOR accounts.

Today, fees are the leading form of agency compensation. According to the Association of National Advertisers' "2013 Trends in Agency Compensation" study, 81% of advertisers use some form of fee-based compensation model such as labor or fixed fees. Commissions have declined rapidly from 15% in 2010 to 5% in 2013. That's 33% less!

Given the pressure on agency compensation and profits, agencies have to think much harder about the value of every potential new client.

Here are three general questions that I think you should get answered ahead of committing to the full-blown agency pitch.

1. What is their marketing communications budget? If they aren't willing to even give you a range, think red flag.

2. How has the client traditionally paid their agencies? Does the client have a preference for cost plus or fixed fee compensation system?

3. Is the client interested in discussing performance-based compensation? After years of discussion, the use of performance incentives has increased dramatically. According to the ANA, performance incentives have increased from 46% in 2010 to 61% in 2013. The top performance criteria are agency performance reviews (75%), brand or awareness metrics (54%), sales goals (48%), profit goals (35%), and brand perception metrics (31%).

I am a fan of performance based compensation or at least factoring performance in some way into the total equation. I realize that establishing performance isn't easy. For years, I worried about not having full-control of my client's marketing programs. How could I be held accountable or rewarded for elements of marketing programs that I didn't have control over? I eventually concluded that it was in my best long-term interest to work with the client to create a compensation system using a combination of fixed fees, agency performance, and bonuses based on meeting or exceeding marketing objectives (awareness, brand share, social media activity, sales). Flexibility is key to writing this type of agreement. Go in thinking that you will be able craft one, and I think you just might get it done.

In fact, having a clearly stated agency compensation plan might accomplish a few pitch-oriented objectives.

You will look professional.

You will probably be one of the very few agencies to have a compensation recommendation to share.

You will use the plan as a neutral discussion-starter.

You will express your interest in the client's success by attaching yours to theirs.

INTERVIEW

Darren Woolley, Founder and Managing Director, TrinityP3

Once again, I turned to Darren Woolley of TrinityP3 for his expert opinion on agency compensation. Or as they say in Australia, remuneration. Regardless of your word choice (and you will see that it is important), how agencies get paid and then make a profit needs to be considered during the agency selection process. Too often agencies wait until they win an account to find out if the account will be profitable.

PL: You work across Asia. Are agencies compensated differently in each country? Is Asia different than Europe or the U.S.?

Darren: The basic methodologies for agency compensation are the same. The application varies across various markets due to culture and government legislation. As you may know, in Brazil, media and creative are legislated to remain together, and the commission system therefore continues to dominate. In India, the commission system is also more common than other markets. But increasingly, the dominant model is the resource-based model as either a retainer or project basis.

The other big difference is the term used. In the UK, and markets previously colonized by the UK, it is called remuneration. While US and US influenced markets call it compensation. While many think the two are synonyms, the fact is they reflect different philosophies. To compensate is to make good for damage or loss. While to remunerate, is to reward for output of effort. To provide the difference, you would never say, "The middle aged executive purchased a new sports car to remunerate for his flagging libido.", would you?

But I think that the use of each reflects a very different underlying philosophy to the payment of agencies for their services and efforts.

PL: What compensation systems are your advertiser clients using?

Darren: The majority of clients are moving to or sticking to a recourse based model using direct salary costs multiplied by the overhead and profit multiple, and divided by the number of annual billable hours in the year. In fact, it is so common that we created a smartphone business app that calculates the cost of resource per hour using this approach or can calculate the salaries from the hourly rate. It is called the TrinityP3 Resource Rate Calculator and is available in all smartphone app stores. This is not an ad, as the app is free.

PL: I am not sure that all agencies understand the difference between fee, resource based, and performance models. Can you help with definitions?

Darren: There is much confusion about many of the terms supporting agency compensation. And the interpretation seems to vary depending on the interests and position of the person using them. Therefore it is important to ensure that all parties to the negotiation are working to the same set of definitions. The definitions we use are as follows:

Fees: This is where a fee is agreed on between the advertiser and the agency for the services provided. These can either be an hourly or daily rate to be applied by role and multiplied by the number of hours or days taken.

Project Fees: This is usually where a project is defined and a project fee with a fixed price is set, usually based on an estimate of the time and resources required, but charged on the output, no matter what the outcome.

Resource Based: This is the most common and is where the cost of the resource provided is based on a formula where the direct salary cost of the resource is multiplied by an agreed overhead and profit multiple to determine the annual fee for the resource, and then divided by the percentage of their time required. This is the underlying approach for most retainer arrangements. It is also considered the 'cost recovery' method because it recovers the agencies largest cost, people, and the associated overhead.

Performance Based: This is where some or all of the agency compensation is put at risk, with payment determined by meeting or delivering a pre-determined set of results or performance criteria. These performance criteria usually fall into one of three categories: Soft (relationship, service delivery, client satisfaction), Medium (marketing and advertising metrics), and Hard (sales and financial performance). I will expand on these below.

Value Based: This is relatively new compared to the other approaches, but basically it is where the advertiser determines a value or price they are willing to pay for specific services and outputs, and the agency works to deliver these within the set price.

PL: Do you see any trends? For example, are you seeing an increased use of performance based compensation models?

Darren: Performance based models are increasingly common, but many struggle with these models in implementation and execution. We have also noticed that some advertisers are moving away from retainers to fees again as they look for more flexible compensation models in the face of less predicable market conditions and therefore, less defined requirements of their agencies.

PL: Many agencies like the theory of performance-based compensation systems but are wary of how these will be calculated. Have you found a way to make this work?

Darren: The problem is that few can get to the balance between risk and reward. The lower the risk, the lower the reward, and so we see as a default that the measures are reduced to the lowest common denominator such as client satisfaction. This has low risk for the agency, but also low value for the advertiser, and so we see this as a performance payment of 5% or 10% of the agency fee. Not a huge incentive, and besides, you end up simply rewarding the agency for doing their job.

But, at the other end is a huge risk for the agency with many factors they cannot directly influence. Then to pay a bonus reward becomes prohibitive, as the budget process most companies use would not allow this level of funding required.

The best situations for performance-based compensation are where the agency or agencies are responsible for direct response. This is increasingly common in the digital domain where consumer behavior can be tracked and the agency rewarded with significant bonuses for delivering increased leads or sales and reducing the cost per acquisition.

PL: What metrics are being used to judge agency success or failures? You've mentioned soft, medium, and hard performance metrics. What are these?

Darren: We see the use of various metrics.

Business Performance (Hard):

> Examples include: sales, traffic, profit, market share, volume growth, etc. These can be measured by the same criteria that the advertiser uses for their internal bonus systems.

> Agencies often claim that business results may not be within their span of control as many factors besides advertising can affect business outcomes.

Advertising Performance (Medium):

> Examples include: product awareness, ad awareness measures, consumer measures, attitude ratings, persuasion, purchase intent, awards, brand equity, image, effectiveness awards, etc.

> This kind of performance assessment is vulnerable to research technique, statistical anomalies, and discussions of creative philosophy.

Agency Performance (Soft):

> Relates to the evaluation of agency functional areas: account services, creative and media in terms of performance, service, relationship, cost efficiencies, etc.

This is highly subjective and may be affected by entertainment on the upside and personality problems on the downside.

PL: Can an agency be paid more for a big business-building idea than just for hours worked?

Darren: There is always an opportunity for agencies to charge for value. The problem is that often the agency and the advertiser's idea of value is misaligned.

Agencies are in the business of ideas and the execution is campaigns, and these are the two areas where they get paid. But for the advertiser, the realization of the value of the big business idea can take months or even years, and the agency wants to be paid now for the idea and not later.

Besides, agencies have been giving away these big business ideas for years as a way to secure the revenue for the implementation and execution. Why should the advertiser start paying for these now?

PL: Scope of work would seem to be a good starting point for compensation discussions. Are clients willing to sit down to discuss scope before budgets are set?

Darren: Scope of work is essential if you are using a resourced based model. How else are you able to determine, with any accuracy, the resource required to deliver the outputs required? The problem is that advertisers are increasingly less inclined to project or commit to a scope of work for their requirements for the coming year as they deal with less certain market movements and increased market complexity.

But we have found that the actual variation is relatively small, year on year. This is because in actual fact the changes in the scope, year on year, still need to be delivered within the marketing budget, which also changes in a defined way. Therefore we have used the previous year's scope of work and adjusted for any overall budget change as a base.

PL: Are retainer models still in use? I could see retainers working best in social media and content creation.

Darren: Retainers are still popular due to their convenience. Think of it as an 'all you can eat' buffet for advertising agencies. But with the change from a campaign or project based services model to an 'always on' model found in social media, SEO, content, and search, the retainer is particularly useful in setting resource expectations and to link these expectations to a scope of work.

PL: Has the use of procurement increased over time? Has this helped or hindered the agency selection process?

Darren: Procurement is more involved than ever before. The involvement of procurement often brings a greater level of discipline and accountability to the process.

When the procurement process is simply applied to reduce agency fees without the required improvements in the advertising and marketing process, it leads to a commoditization of the core value creation in the process, the human resources within the agencies.

Instead of simply focusing on costs, where the procurement team focuses on process improvement, performance management, and developing ROI methodologies, the cost reduction is driven by greater efficiencies and proven value creation.

PL: Agencies have complained that they are asked to pitch before knowing how the client is going to compensate the agency. Do your clients set and discuss budgets during the pitch process? If not, why not?

Darren: Under a confidentiality agreement, we always reveal the size of the potential engagement either in fees, budget, or an approximation of FTEs. Many marketers and procurement people are concerned with this approach, as they feel it is revealing too much to the agencies. But for us, it is the ideal way to set agency expectations, so they are better able to decide how much to invest in time, money, and resources to win the business. It is a business decision after all.

PL: Finally, can there be a perfect client and agency compensation model? I miss the days of the 15% media commission. It made life so simple, and of course, highly profitable for agencies.

Darren: The world is a much more complex place than the 1960s reflected in Mad Men. There is no longer a one size fits all. Certainly there are preferred models such as retainers and fees, but all of these have failings, driving marketers, procurement, and agencies to find better and improved models. This is complicated even further by the driving change of technology and the impact it is having on consumer behavior and the media. So in a word, while you may miss the old days of 15% media commission, no – the world is no longer one size fits all anymore.

———

Legal And Intellectual Property Issues

As an agency owner and business development director, I have been, like many of you, concerned about giving away valuable ideas in new business pitches. After all, ideas are the most valuable intellectual property an agency has to offer their clients.

One of the more vexing questions is: Who owns our ideas once we've presented them in a pitch?

The spec issue.

In Chapter 5, I discuss my views on presenting spec creative. I have always had mixed feelings about spec work, but my personal history suggests that my batting average is higher when I've presented work. I think that this is due to the simple fact that on paper, most agencies look and sound alike. Spec work, which also includes strategic insights, can separate an agency from the other presenting agencies, and the work just might dazzle the client into giving you the account.

To present spec or not is a very personal decision for most agencies. The decision is driven by the fear that another agency is going to go all out, and then you won't look as interested in the client's business, or conversely, they held back, and you gave up a brilliant idea for nothing. Alternatively, some agencies are so hot and/or principled that they simply refuse to do any spec work.

There are times when a client will directly ask for spec work. The bad news is that this often feels like overreaching and an indication that the client isn't capable of selecting an agency based on agency history. However, as search consultants point out, clients occasionally ask for spec to just to witness and take part in an agency's creative process.

Final point. If a client tells you that whatever you present will be their property, I'd quickly back away. Excuse my language but – WTF? At best, (if there is a best case), you at least know that the other agencies are in the same position.

INTERVIEW
Sharon Toerek, Partner, Toerek Law

The issues surrounding the ownership of ideas or intellectual property are complex. To help us all get a better understanding of these new business issues and intellectual property (IP) ownership, copyright law, NDA's, and general client and agency agreements, I turned to an expert. The following interview first appeared on the Advertising Week Social Club website in 2013.

Sharon Toerek is an advertising, marketing, and intellectual property attorney at Cleveland's Toerek Law. Sharon's national practice concentrates on assisting her marketing communications clients protect, enforce, and monetize their creative assets. She has spoken to the advertising community at various events including Advertising Age's Small Agency Conference.

PL: Can you help us understand what intellectual property means?

Sharon: Intellectual property is actually an umbrella term for the legal protections associated with various kinds of intellectual capital. It covers trademarks, which are the legal underpinning for brand identities, including names, logos, and taglines for brands. It covers copyright, which is a 'bundle' of legal rights to any creative product that you can look at or touch, whether it is graphic design, photography, video, or a mobile app – including the right to copy it, license it, or sell it to others for use. It also covers patents, which are increasingly being utilized in the ad world as agencies develop original proprietary tech solutions. It rarely includes 'ideas', unless the parties involved have some sort of confidentiality agreement in place that protects the information – and even then, it might be protected, but still not actually be intellectual property.

PL: How does one secure and prove ownership of IP?

Sharon: It depends on the type of IP.

Protecting a trademark for a brand is fairly straightforward – you want to make sure it is legally clear before it is adopted and that the brand owner files for federal trademark registration and then monitors its brands for infringement problems.

Copyright is more challenging because there are so many layers of copyright in any finished product that an agency turns out for its client. At a high level, proper copyright notices on deliverables and federal copyright registrations for completed works where appropriate are good tools to protect copyright. It's also critical where multiple 'creators' are involved to have written agreements in place that say who will own which rights and under what circumstances – US copyright law requires agreements in writing in these circumstances.

PL: Is the concept of IP different in the advertising and design world than in other industries?

Sharon: The legal principles are the same regardless of the industry, but I will say the ad and marketing industries have the somewhat unique situation of what I will call 'virtual creation', which is the longstanding practice of using a combination of agency partners, freelancers, specialty vendors, and sometimes client in-house resources to all contribute to the end product – whether it's a commercial, a social media campaign, or print work. There is almost never just one creator, which means that copyright is all over the place. Folks in the creative services world frequently don't take the time to document these transactions in writing, which causes copyright ownership issues later.

The other issue I see frequently is a failure to properly clear or perform due diligence for brand marks before they're being adopted. I see a lot of the following situations: neither the agency or client do any due diligence or clearance, *or* the agency and client focus on obtaining cool domain names and substitute this process for the trademark clearance process, or everyone knows trademark is an issue but they get started with the process after they are already far down the expensive path of executing the new brand…which sometimes creates really unpleasant and expensive trademark outcomes.

PL: What unique issues confront advertising agencies in the area of IP ownership?

Sharon: Agencies are sometimes direct creators and also sometimes traffic managers or navigators of the creation process if they are managing virtual teams or vendor partners to get the client what it needs. They have lots of buckets of creative product to manage rights around. They're also in the best position to keep everyone aware of the potential IP issues in the branding or creative processes, even if they defer the actual legal due diligence to the vendors' or client's teams.

The other very challenging IP ownership hot button for agencies is ownership of IP created during the new business process. Closely related to that is the question of fair compensation for IP created during the new business process, whether it's spec work (which we're seeing less and less of, thankfully) or simply concepts or ideation.

PL: Advertising agencies are in the idea business. Is it true that nobody owns an idea?

Sharon: That is actually quite true if the idea is expressed freely without any confidentiality arrangement in place to protect the communication of it.

There are two ways to protect an idea – keep it to yourself (not practical in a business development situation or in the creative process), or don't disclose it without a nondisclosure agreement (NDA). That doesn't mean agencies can't do a few things to protect misappropriation of their work. Copyright principles can be very helpful protection in a new business situation as long as your ideas are expressed in some physical form – like storyboards, written proposals, work scope descriptions, or video. Once your agency is actually engaged, the language in your agreement is crucial to keep everyone on the same page about who owns which IP and when.

PL: How does the idea ownership issue effect new business pitches?

Sharon: It's critical. This is one of the top legal hot button issues agency leaders worry about. They want to be invited to the table, but be fairly treated for their ideation during a new business pitch. And they want these things without ticking off the prospective client, which makes the discussion sensitive. So many times, they are just not addressing it and taking a leap of faith that their great ideas will lead to the paid gig that makes the IP ownership not as crucial of a concern.

PL: What can agencies do to protect themselves? We often feel very vulnerable.

Sharon: I know – it's tricky for agencies. There are a few things. Sometimes working out an NDA is a practical solution, especially if it is a mutual NDA. The agency will keep the prospective client's information confidential, and in consideration, the prospect will keep confidential the communications and ideas expressed by the agency during the pitch process. When you approach it from a place of mutual fairness and communicate that to the prospect, it can work.

If it doesn't, you have 3 additional choices. One is to walk away, which is sometimes the right move. Another is to take the leap of faith, and make the investment of time and money that goes along with that leap, and chalk it up to a lesson learned if the pitch doesn't lead to the client work – but at least you are doing so after careful consideration and with very open eyes. That is also a valid business decision. A third choice is to negotiate the ownership rights in advance, which increasingly prospective clients are willing to do. It's never enough money to make the agency whole for the investment made in the pitch, but allows at least some investment recovery, and again, at least the agency knows where it stands on the ownership question and makes a choice about it in advance.

PL: What power do ad agencies have?

Sharon: Well they certainly have the power of demanding clarity on the IP rights issue from a prospect in advance of the pitch.

Being vocal as an agency community on the IP ownership issue has also been more helpful than most agencies probably realize. It was just a few short years ago that extensive spec work for a marketer, including the prospect's ownership of the spec work for no compensation, was standard operating procedure in new business pitch. And it only takes a few willing agencies to feed that expectation in the industry. But increasingly, agencies have declined those pitch terms with prospects, and it is resulting in far less uncompensated spec work being done during the new business process.

Agencies are also becoming more savvy about creating their own proprietary solutions and licensing, not selling, them to clients to create recurring revenue streams from their IP. They're also being firmer about requiring renegotiation with clients who want to expand the scope of permitted uses of creative product.

PL: Is it important to have an NDA? Do you find that marketers are willing to sign these?

Sharon: I find that more marketers are willing to have those conversations if they're approached from a place of mutuality. I would be overstating if I claimed that marketers like to sign them – I would say that we're seeing less overreaching by marketers on this issue than we were seeing a few years ago. I would also be overstating if I said that it's a completely level playing field out there – it isn't. The marketers have the budgets, and at the end of the day, creative agencies' currency is their ability to monetize their creative product.

PL: Are there any other points that should be negotiated?

Sharon: Agencies, especially independent smaller agencies, sometimes need to push back on the errors and omissions insurance demands. It isn't that an agency should go without this coverage – it should not – but more that the policy limits need to be more reasonable. I've seen very high E&O demands to small agencies from large marketers that just don't make sense in light of the work scope.

Another area where agencies should be careful is on the restrictive covenants sometimes demanded by marketers. It's usually fair to agree that you won't work with a direct competitor of the client. It's usually less fair to be required to stay out of an industry entirely unless you have an AOR relationship or very significant project engagement. It's very unfair to allow the client to directly recruit and hire your key employees for internal creative roles and cut the agency out of the relationship – they've only been exposed to the client's brand, culture, and work because of the agency-marketer relationship, so a defined "hands off" period frequently makes sense.

———

Chemistry and Presentation Dynamics

By now, you've seen that there are many ways that an agency can win or lose a pitch.

However, there seems to be one aspect of pitching that keeps coming up over and over and rises to the top of almost everyone's list. That is the idea that agencies ultimately win or lose based on interpersonal chemistry and corporate culture alignment.

My fear with the *chemistry thing* is that it can appear to be something that just is vs. something that can be managed and created. There is a school of thought that says that you either gel with the prospect, or you don't. Sorry Ms. Agency Business Development Director, it's all about a chemical reaction, and that's why it is called chemistry.

Yikes. After preparing a smart, tight presentation, are we ultimately at the mercy and vagaries of some mysterious and unmanageable *human thing*? Pheromones, anyone?

I refuse to think that we don't have any control. I don't like the idea that after the long and expensive journey from an agency's business development outreach to RFI's, RFP's, and then on to the final presentation, it all comes down to fate: the client either digs you, or they don't. It just sounds way too passive.

So what can we do to build chemistry?

Let's start with what *not* to do. Do not make any of the mistakes discussed in preceding chapters. Think of it this way: if you are twenty something and you are going out to find your mate, you shower and dress accordingly. If you are a surfer, you wear Hurley's. If you work on Wall Street, you wear Prada. Once you've defined your target prospect (yes, this is a book about marketing after all) and aligned persona's, you know that you need to do the obvious: make eye contact and act interested in the other person's story. You will try to avoid any conversation-killing words. Even better, you will lean in and listen and make adjustments to your side of the conversation to demonstrate your interest. You won't bore them with endless stories that are all about you. You will flatter them.

OK, you get it. Avoid the things that you *can* control. Yes, I believe we can.

But can we manufacture and/or control interpersonal chemistry? Or, is it just up to some form of business pheromones?

New business chemistry gets even more complicated when you introduce the idea that chemistry must be built between two groups in addition to individuals. Sure, some pitches are won because of an agency's charismatic leader. However, in most cases it is your team that is being evaluated.

In order to develop chemistry between two separate groups (clients and agency presenters), the presenter group, *as a whole*, needs to demonstrate an understanding of the client group's challenges, a commonality of purpose, matching emotional commitment (passion), empathy for shared problems, and a common language. Ultimately you will build rapport with the client group if they think that you are all in sync, as in on the same wavelength, especially in understanding their business issues. This is one of the reasons that you always need to remember that the pitch is much more about them, not you.

Two key words to keep on the top of your mind and manage are *values*, as in having and demonstrating shared values, and *trust*, as in building confidence in your agency's integrity and reliability. Building trust is particularly important in service pitches where the client will be committing to a personal relationship. Trust is more easily given between two similar groups; groups that have already established commonalities. You are like me, therefore I understand you better and can trust you more easily.

Cultural alignment is also critical. Assuming that there isn't a total disconnect between the client's values and yours (this is something you should have figured out back at the RFP stage), cultural alignment can be managed. To get there, make sure ahead of any meeting that you read up on the client's Mission and Vision Statements, review their brand values, and understand their corporate goals. If the client is a public company, read their annual report. It provides a comprehensive overview of the company's business and financial condition and their dreams.

Find commonalties between the client and your agency, and subtly reinforce these in the meeting. As I mentioned earlier, my ex-client Sara Lee's Mission Statement states that they want: "To simply delight you… every day." Surely your agency could find a very creative way to mirror the idea of "delight" in your pitch and even (very sparingly) use the word "delight" to reinforce rapport.

To help further understand chemistry management and presentation dynamics, I turned to two presentation and interpersonal experience experts, Nancy Duarte and Debra Weekley.

INTERVIEW
Nancy Duarte, Principal, Duarte, Inc.

Nancy Duarte is a leading communication expert. Her firm, Duarte, Inc., is the global leader behind some of the most influential visual messaging in business and culture.

Nancy is the author of three award winning books. *Resonate: Present Visual Stories that Transform Audiences* identifies the hidden story structures inherent in great communication, and it spent more than 300 days on Amazon's top 100 business book bestsellers list. *Slide:ology: The Art and Science of Creating Great Presentations* teaches readers to think visually and has been translated into eight languages. The *HBR Guide to Persuasive Presentations: Inspire action, engage the audience to sell your ideas* is a presentation guidebook.

PL: Chemistry between the advertising agency and the prospective client is generally considered the most important factor in agency selection. What are the best methods for presenters to build chemistry with their audiences?

Nancy: Good working chemistry is important between a client and services firm. The best way to have chemistry is to do your homework about the person you're talking to and their company. You need to know the brand and know the client, *really* know them.

Do that by researching them as individuals as well as the external factors that influence them. Look them up online, look at their social media feeds to see their interests, see if they've been cited in articles or have strong personal interests. Also, the moment you know you'll be presenting, set up news alerts for them and the company so you can also see what the market is saying about the company and what pressures they may be under. I do all this for a high-stakes presentation. If you can get to the point where you know them well, you'll present to them like you're speaking to a friend and not a stranger.

But don't let them know you've researched them; it could creep them out.

PL: Single presenters like Steve Jobs can control all elements of a presentation. Agency pitches are usually a team effort. Do you have any tips for agencies for managing how multiple presenters should work together during presentations? (Some issues include varying degrees of experience, presentation flow, and seamless person to person hand offs.)

Nancy: Steve Jobs rarely presented on the stage alone. He always had people coming and going during his talk, and they usually delivered an important piece of information. Since Jobs is a master communicator, usually the other folks invited to speak aren't as amazing as he was, yet the audience was comfortable with that contrast. In an agency pitch, obviously, everyone needs to be a contributor of sorts or they probably shouldn't attend the meeting. It needs to be rehearsed like a tight jazz ensemble. The junior people can present, just make sure that what they say is clear and adds value.

One thing we do is brainstorm every way the clients might derail the pitch or resist the pitch. Having less experienced people in that brainstorm would prepare them to be ready for any surprises.

PL: Often agencies have to include inexperienced subject matter experts or junior staff in presentations. What efficient methods can organizations use to train and prepare inexperienced staff?

Nancy: At Duarte we hold a communication workshop twice a year. Each workshop is two hours a week for six weeks. Our employees learn how to shape an idea and represent their idea in a compelling way. Some employees take the course every year. As a firm that specializes in presentations, we all have to be presenters.

———

I next turned to an expert in agency business and team relationships.

INTERVIEW
Debra Weekley - Principle at Connectivenergy, LLC

Debra Weekley's career includes Fortune 500 account management at Wieden+Kennedy and Saatchi & Saatchi. After her agency career, she took that time-honored leap to the client side and served in marketing and human resources leadership positions at Nike.

Debra helps creative and entrepreneurial companies better connect as a team, with their markets, and welcome change to deliver their best work. A consistent thread throughout her work is insightful, thoughtful, and creative facilitation. Her focus is on personal, interpersonal, team, and leadership development. One of her passions is helping younger professionals navigate this very competitive marketplace, as they become managers and leaders.

PL: How do you define personal chemistry?

Deb: Personal chemistry is magical and a bit scientific. Magically, there are people with whom I immediately feel a strong attraction, a common bond and they make me want to jump right into deep engagement: they 'get me,' I 'get them'. It's memorable, immediate, and profound. Overtime, an important trust develops. Research shows that establishing similarity between people is a critical component of chemistry. A few other core components are mutual trust, empathy, being non-judgmental, and effortless communication. If the goal is to develop lasting partnerships, it is important to go even further. *Feeling understood* is an essential piece of establishing good relationships.

This is true in new business pitches where the agency has to demonstrate that they are strategically aligned with the client.

PL: How can chemistry between groups be managed or even rehearsed ahead of a presentation?

Deb: Chemistry happens when people are attracted to one another. Usually, it's because the other person or team provides something vital for them around something very important. Group chemistry, or group cohesion, happens when a varied group of people works together and make a united effort to accomplish the goals and objectives of the collective whole, like meeting specific marketing objectives. I think diversity a group is healthy and vital. Diversity, by definition, involves people of very different backgrounds, ways of thinking, and preferences in communications. Once this diversity is aligned towards a common cause (like memorable work on behalf of a client), chemistry kicks in.

Good group chemistry can be both learned and improved with clear communication and practice.

PL: Is there a way for an agency pitch team to act as a unit or will agencies always be dependent on the power of a charismatic leader like a Dan Wieden?

Deb: I think the best unit usually wins. This team has thoughtfully crafted an approach and smart options that show depth, breadth, and unique connection with the consumer. Most agencies have some sort of media-darling CEO, Star or spokesperson, but it's the team that usually wins the pitch. I've often been in a situation where the Star can take a pitch to the point where the client is highly interested, but the client then engages with the rest of the team to find out if the initial love fest is sustainable through media planning, production, and even financial systems.

Dan Wieden is smart, skilled, and powerful with potential clients, and he works well in a team. At W+K we always agreed to our specific roles before pitches and picked our teams to best align with what we knew about our potential clients. We were very careful to not trot out people, agency super stars, that the client would never see again. Besides Dan's prescient, thoughtful brain, I think his biggest gift is his amazing listening skill. He listens and actually cares what a client, a market, or a community is REALLY saying. Having the agency CEO really listen inspires trust. Then, Dan can deliver his magic.

PL: Are there tools or exercises that an agency team can use to build their chemistry?

Deb: Yes, although it's important to note that most off-the-shelf tools are designed to work with big corporations, because that's where all the money is. I finally found one that works for smaller creative groups while I was at Nike. It's an effectiveness system called Insights Discovery. It's based on Jungian psychology and connects well with creative teams because it's very visual, fun, and memorable… like many ads I know.

Agency chemistry is also very important. From my days as a client, I can tell you that it's quite apparent when a team doesn't have it's own chemistry: you don't want to buy people who don't respect each other's differences and don't trust one another. Agencies are paid to have healthy team dynamics. The pitch must demonstrate this.

PL: How can an agency find the chemistry hot-buttons in a client organization?

Deb: The first thing to do is to ensure that all agency members really, really know themselves: their key value to the team, strengths, weaknesses, and communications preferences. Once people understand themselves, they can better identify when their own personal 'lens' might be getting in the way of a potential client connection.

PL: Can big-brained but *introverted* Creative people ever become compelling presenters?

Deb: Never try to change big-brained introverted Creative professionals. Their ability to listen, ponder the between-the-lines meaning, and then concoct a creative solution to a boring brief is powerful.

What you can do is take them (and other team members surrounding the Creative Director) through a training program so all learn how to better connect and adapt to someone who isn't like them. Some of the best account managers I've known have been very Creative people who mastered the ability to connect and adapt their own style to the client and/or situation. Learning how to connect and adapt isn't always easy and requires practice. This needs to be done well ahead of the pressure that comes from an imminent pitch.

———

Strategy

An endless series of marketing client research studies help advertising agencies understand what keeps marketers up at night. Sleepless nights come from agencies that don't take the time to understand the client's business objectives, don't exhibit client – agency alignment, don't generate ideas, don't keep up with the shifting digital world, and can't help determine the ROI of marketing programs. Most, if not all, of these issues show up in RFP's and pitch briefs.

While all of these issues should be addressed across the entire agency from account management to media planning to mobile marketing, sleep-generating solutions most often come in the form of agency strategic thinking.

When I first moved to London in the early 1990's, I had the pleasure of entering the golden age of account planning. Even New York agencies hadn't truly grasped the benefits of planners. One of the definitions of account planning is that it brings the consumer mindset into the process of developing advertising. Here are two more definitions that directly relate to most client pitches.

"The account planner is that member of the agency's team who is the expert, through background, training, experience, and attitudes, at working with information and getting it used – not just marketing research but all the information available to help solve a client's advertising problems."

- Stanley Pollitt, founder Boase Massimi Pollitt and wrote the book, *Pollitt On Planning.*

"Planners are involved and integrated in the creation of marketing strategy and ads. Their responsibility is to bring the consumer to the forefront of the process and to inspire the team to work with the consumer in mind. The planner has a point of view about the consumer and is not shy about expressing it."

- Lisa Fortini-Campbell, Kellogg School of Management

Earlier in the book, I discussed that the Internet has helped us all become more adept at research and being able to deliver many of the benefits of account planning. That said, being an expert in strategic planning and innovation is a full-time job. Here is one of the full-time experts.

INTERVIEW
Faris Yakob, Founder and Principle, Genius|Steals

Faris Yakob is the Founder and Principle of Genius|Steals a global planning, idea and innovation consultancy that works on new product concepts, new communication ideas, workshops, inspiration, strategy, content creation, and new ways of thinking. Genius|Steals' clients include: Fast Company, Grey Advertising, Marriott, Microsoft, Ogilvy (NY), and P&G.

Prior to founding Genius|Steals, he was Chief Innovation Officer MDC Partners/KBS+ and EVP Chief Technology Strategist at McCann Erickson.

To top it off, among other kudos, Faris was Chairman of Integrated Jury and Content&Contact Jury at the 2011 Clio Awards.

PL: Do you call yourself an account planner?

Faris: That's a good question. I have been an account planner, a media planner, a digital strategist, a communications strategist, and I've been a management consultant. So I guess, loosely in the area of strategy, I'd say yes.

PL: Going with that, what would you say is the role of an account planner or strategist in the process of developing a new client pitch?

Faris: I make a distinction between a strategist and an account planner as being in different stages in the process. The way I usually encapsulate it is that a strategy informs the need for advertising, whereas an account planner will inform the advertising.

They're slightly different parts of the process. The account planner assumes we're going do ads, and the strategist looks for the right solution to a problem, which may involve advertising in its traditional sense. The strategist directs the solution to a problem in the most effective way.

An account planner's historical role has been to be the voice of the consumer inside the advertising agency and to be responsible for the efficacy of work. The planner makes sure the work works – to give a fundamentally subjective creative product the best possible chance of a commercial success.

PL: How does that work in a pitch environment where a presentation's being developed in a very short period of time?

Faris: It's the same as any kind of creative pitching process in my opinion, which is initially, the gathering and distillation of the largest, most relevant set of sources that might impact the solution. Sources include context, movements in culture, historical efficacy of past work, and all brands in the set. It's the distillation and chemical interpretation of lots and lots of data observation into the most useful, salient, densely generative aspects of that data.

There's a tendency typical of big advertising agencies to use research as validation as well in that process. They use very rapid turnaround quantitative and qualitative research to support the validation of ideas (i.e. the drunk who uses a lamppost for support).

I'm less enamored, let's say, with use of this type of research, because I fundamentally don't think that showing somebody a comp and saying "Would you buy more toilet paper if I showed you this cartoon of a bear?" is very useful accept as theatrical validation, but that's not the point I guess. Or is the point, I guess.

PL: You are well schooled in digital strategy. Are there digital tools, in the best case off the shelf tools, that help you unearth insights?

Faris: A hundred percent. The first place I would start usually is Google. And I don't mean that in the tritest sense. One of the things I've been baffled by when consulting with a wealth of agencies (until quite recently), is the lack of using Google search terms as the starting point of market analysis of changing trends.

One of the first things I do to understand the marketplace, for example, is to use Google Trends to understand market share. How does the market operate? What are the smallest delineations of that market? What do we consider the successful set, and how do the players in that set operate? So search traffic and volume tends to mirror market share almost exactly in every case that I've seen. That's one of the first things you have to look at.

Google gives you lots of interesting information immediately: what the market's like in terms of the brands operating within it, what their relative positions are, and how they're moving. That's rather important.

A corollary of that tool is that Google gives you recommendations of words that are search allies: words that strongly correlate in search queries with those terms. So just looking at that you begin to see what words are most associated via search with a brand, or the topic, et cetera. And it also shows you words that are declining in relevance and those gaining in relevance at the time. You can see trends in that category, trends in that marketplace, as things become more or less salient based entirely on search volume. So that's one thing.

I also use online qualitatively as well. I look at social platforms and find real people saying real things about a topic. I get a selection of opinions that is somewhat representative.

PL: In this case you are going online, into the world of social media, and you are listening to what consumers are saying and discussing in the marketplace?

Faris: Absolutely. One of the great things about social media is that people talk about everything: the corpus of data is now very large. You can, with some basic search tools and platforms, find interesting nuggets of actual speech. I find this valuable because historically the only way we could access actual speech was to put people in a focus group room and show them materials and then ask questions. That framework is incredibly fraught with methodical bias. Focus groups or interviews have to be very carefully undertaken by very skilled people, in my opinion, to not let the methods of research completely dictate the answers. How you ask the questions dictates the answers in many cases.

PL: You are now able to get a more authentic answer or insight? Is that one way to put it?

Faris: Yes. You get a more *real* piece of speech than you would in the context of a direct interrogation about a brand or category.

PL: Thinking of a pitch situation itself, is there a best time to do a reveal of a big idea? Is the reveal better in the front, the middle, or the back? When is the "ah-ha" moment?

Faris: There are a number of different approaches to this, and I have to say it's variable. It depends entirely on, hopefully, how you understand the client and their need for working together. There is a school of thought which says bringing the client in early and pre-selling them on half the idea is a good practice. Sometimes I have to fight for that early meeting, although I also think that on some occasions chemistry meetings can be artificial and weirdly awkward.

I think it's about building a journey or a way of building a scaffold. So when the idea appears, it seems both obvious and necessary, rather than "ta-da!"

When does it come? Again, that's interesting too. It depends on how you articulate what the idea is and the difference between the idea and executions of the idea. I remember when I worked briefly with Alex Bogusky, and he told the tale of the Burger King pitch. He said they didn't present the first television script until over two and a half hours in because they wanted to demonstrate they weren't just a TV agency – that they were thinking strategically about the product and the problem and so forth. There should be a strategy to address the cadence of a pitch, and it depends on what you're trying to impress somebody with. I think the idea of the big idea is challenging now because there's a lot of components that we're looking at. It's not just a thought or a line necessarily: it's something that informs a creative tonality in the solution's architecture.

PL: Clients are immersed in their brand, their consumers, and their markets. Is there any way to know in advance that your idea, your big idea, your insight, the wonderful thing that you've uncovered, is something that hasn't been previously uncovered?

Faris: I think yes and no. The first thing obviously is for you to distill all the client's documents and read between the lines of the briefing documents, because they tend to, strictly working with large clients, just give you reams and reams of deckage. And so lots of information will be in there that looks like the beginnings of insight.

The thing is with both insight and ideas, the first set of things you think about any problem are always going be the most obvious. That's how brains work. The most obvious set of combinations, which is what ideas tend to be, swim around the problems. As soon as you say "burgers", your brain has a number of associations that it begins to bring up really rapidly. The challenge then is to get beyond those to the least obvious insight, the least obvious idea. In some sense it's the most creative and therefore the least likely to be seen before. I guess it's impossible to know with an experienced client that they haven't seen the insight before. But, hopefully you append your idea with something very recent that exists in the world that's relevant, to get to something modern rather than obvious.

PL: Interesting, so even if the idea pre-exists, there might be a different way to express it and use it based on recency.

Faris: Yes, exactly.

I think one of the biggest questions in marketing today is what should we do with an idea in an infinite possible array of channels and executions? What's the right thing to do? What's strategically most likely to achieve the success that you're looking for is part of the challenge.

I also think, to your previous question, there's a certain a way of discussing an idea that just involves bravery on the part of the agency.

In Jon Steel's book, *Truth, Lies, and Advertising*, he talks about the only insight they took into a Porsche pitch. Research showed that for many people when they are sitting in a car next to a Porsche, they are looking at the driver and thinking "what an asshole". And that was Porsche's big problem – Porsche drivers were considered to be assholes. Porsche had to do a lot of work to adjust that perception. So I guess that kind of bravery also tends to be less common or obvious when presenting to clients.

PL: What would you consider your best moment in a pitch? Have there have been some wonderful, exciting, "this is it", "this is how life should be" moments?

Faris: Yes, I've had a couple of really pleasant ones. Early on, I was working at Naked in Sydney, and the office was only nine people at the time. We were invited to pitch Telstra, which is the biggest company in Australia. It's a telecoms monopoly in the manner of AT&T before the breakup. It owns the Internet service provider, the telecom company, and the biggest mobile network. It's a huge company that has perception issues, as monopolies often do, because it doesn't necessarily invest in innovation. We were a very small company, yet Telstra invited us to pitch against large incumbent agencies. We found ourselves in our little office with this massive row of clients crammed in sort of a boardroom. Winning seemed incredibly unlikely, but we found out the next day that we had won a piece of the business. It had just seemed incredibly unlikely.

That was the moment when I realized that the cool thing about our industry is that sometimes, if you go in and tell a better story and come up with a better solution, you can win.

PL: Was that a function of personal chemistry and ideas? Or, just the ideas?

Faris: I think it's a combination of the two and that Naked had a different approach than traditional agencies, and… we were charming.

I think that one of the big problems agencies have is differentiation. Many agencies refuse to make choices. Steve Henry, one of the founders of HHCL in London, wrote an article a couple years ago about the lack of values agencies now have. He used an expression from Groucho Marx: "These are my beliefs. If you don't like them, I have others.", which is what he said was so wrong about agencies.

PL: I have one more question. What do you see as the biggest mistake that agencies make when pitching?

Faris: One I've seen repeatedly in working on massive RFP pitches with big ad agencies is the agency's complete ability to ignore the RFP's requirements entirely. It's happened repeatedly in ad agencies in America and elsewhere. The mistake is selling what you sell rather than providing a solution that the client asks for.

PL: It is always amazing to hear that some agencies don't listen or follow directions. Not the best way to approach closing the deal when clients are looking for agencies that actually listen.

———

The Agency Perspective

Hey, Levitan. Enough already about your agency perspective. What do other agency managers think? Yeah, yeah, I figured that you, dear reader, had reached this point in the book.

Here are the perspectives on pitching from an agency search and selection thought leader at the 4A's, an agency network CEO (who got to sit on the client's side of the table), and,the CEO of a London advertising agency. I think that it's a great mix.

Three Advertising Agency Opinions from Tom Finneran, Tony Mikes and Michael Moszynski

INTERVIEW
Tom Finneran: EVP, Agency Management Services – The 4A's

Tom Finneran leads the 4A's Agency Management Services team which provides industry guidance, member consultation, and benchmark information in the areas of new business, agency compensation, agency management, and operations.

Tom's career includes extensive ad agency and advertiser financial management experience. He was executive Vice president/CFO at Jordan McGrath Case & Partners and Arnold McGrath Worldwide, a unit of Havas. He was also Executive Vice President/COO at Grey's promotional unit, J. Brown/LMC.

PL: While there's no one-size-fits-all pitch process, do you think that clients are running more professional pitches today than in the past?

Tom: What we consistently hear is that reviews have become less professional and efficient than in the past. This is important because, to a degree clients have taken in-house some of the review practices that have traditionally been managed by industry consultants who were more adept at running professional pitches.

In terms of the efficiency of reviews, some of the things that are less efficient than they should be are cattle calls. You'll have clients who are not experienced at doing reviews, and they'll send information requests to far more agencies than should be included in the initial list.

Some of the other inefficient processes are what I would refer to as RFPs from hell. Here is one example. About a year and a half ago, one of our members called irate about an RFP that had 300 questions. And I said, "You've got to be exaggerating. It couldn't possibly have been 300 questions." So the person said, "Wait a minute. Let me look at this." Then she commented, "Okay. You got me, I exaggerated. It's 293 questions." So this was an RFP that a client-sourcing group used. The RFP was geared to soliciting responses from ingredient suppliers, research and development firms, and contractors of all types. And woven into the 293 questions were a few marketing-related questions that were kind of like packed in there.

PL: So are you seeing these kinds of issues primarily with larger clients or also medium-sized to smaller clients?

Tom: These tended to be from marketers who did not have dedicated, knowledgeable marketing procurement folks. They were taking people who could source corrugated materials and chemical components and things of that nature.

PL: Is there an agency size factor? Is it affecting your large and small 4A's members?

Tom: It affects members both small and large.

PL: Is that what you currently see as the biggest efficiency problem?

Tom: No. I have a list of efficiency problems I'd like to go through.
One is cattle calls.
Two is RFPs from hell.
Three is the sub-optimal use of RFIs. Too many clients start a review with requests for detailed proposals when, in point of fact, they should be using a streamlined RFI to vet the long list. Get it down to a manageable few. And then start the deeper dive, including an RFP. Going out with an RFP to 10, 12, 15, or God knows how many more is just not an efficient process. So we recommend starting that long list phase with an RFI.

PL: Do you think clients are doing this out of, let's call it naiveté, or are they sometimes fishing for ideas?

Tom: There are certainly instances of clients conducting a review and fishing for ideas. There's no question about that.

PL: You and the ANA put together a fairly extensive pitch guidelines document. How are you getting that document into the hands of clients so that hopefully they'll run better pitches in the future?

Tom: The 4A's and the ANA have actually collaborated on two documents, and I would view them as two chapters of the same book. A couple of years ago we authored guidelines for agency search. About a year or so after those guidelines were released, we wanted to understand if people were adhering to the guidelines. Are they making a difference, and what are the challenges that are still out there?

The challenges we heard back were sub-optimal use of RFIs, RFPs from hell, and inadequate briefings. So based on that, we again collaborated with the ANA and released just late last year, an agency selection briefing guide that advocates the broader use of RFIs. It describes when an RFI should be used and the advantages of using it. And it talks about the necessity of having a thorough briefing for every submission for review.

One point we have not yet addressed is the importance of having a client management decision-maker involved throughout the process.

Another is that we're seeing more and more project reviews. So instead of a review for a major AOR or retainer relationship, these are reviews just for a short-term project and clearly the industry needs to do some work on streamlining processes and procedures for project reviews.

I wanted to get back to your specific question of "What are we doing to get the word out?" We introduced the second set of guidance during Advertising Week 2013. We have been communicating through ANA to their members using everything from bulletins, to a member webinar, and at the ANA Finance and Procurement Conference.

PL: Are you finding that your member agencies are disseminating this document to their prospective clients as well?

Tom: We are. And it's to that fact we urge members to proactively utilize these guidelines. So as soon as they hear about a potential review, we are urging our members to send to the marketer these guidelines and to use the document as a trigger to discuss with the marketer how they're going to conduct their reviews, what they're really looking for, what the elements of the process will be. Some agencies are better than others at directly asking the marketer to provide any examples of where their process might appear to be varied from the industry guidelines.

By the way, the feedback that the proactive agencies have gotten has been universally positive. It's because the proactive nature of the agency talking about, "Well how are you going do this?" rather than just saying, "Oh great, there's going be a review, can I get in?" is viewed as more professional, thoughtful and diligent.

PL: Well I think that's a great insight. I always thought that ultimately the client is not in the business of torture. The key point I heard in your answer is that savvy agencies recognize that they look more professional when they can help the client be more efficient with their search process.

Tom: Exactly right.

In terms of getting the word out, Microsoft, which recently announced the conclusion of their agency review, initially contacted Nancy Hill, the President of the 4A's, and asked about the guidelines that we had on agency searching. That is not an uncommon circumstance where marketers will contact us at an early stage.

PL: Well let me shift this conversation just slightly. I wanted to get your opinion on something that my research into presentations and the whole pitch process revealed. It's sort of obvious that, to a certain extent, once agencies have gone through the RFI and RFP process there's a similarity between the agencies. Do you have any insights as to how

member agencies are working to separate themselves from the pack? Let's say during a presentation? How do they do that?

Tom: Actually, one differentiator that is becoming more and more apparent, and is becoming a key-determining factor in agency selection, is cultural compatibility. And that's borne out, in part, in our work with the ANA on guidance. We added a whole supplement about cultural compatibility. In the review process, agencies that have particularly strong cultures make sure that they are able to engage with the client in ways so the client knows about the agency's cultural expectations, the agency's values and beliefs, the way the agency expects to work with clients, and the way the agency expects to be treated. It carries over into the way agencies prepare for and conduct final presentations.

The best example of this is The Richards Group, who will not participate in a review unless, at some point during the process, the client agrees to go to Dallas. That is an ironclad rule, and they will not deviate from it. The reason Stan and the Richards Group picked that stance is that they have certain ways of working and established agency philosophies. They need the client to come to Dallas to meet them in their own space, and understand the way they operate. This attention to cultural compatibility carries through in the way that they conduct themself within a review. And The Richards Group has a pretty admirable new business record.

PL: I'm hearing you say that the *right* client will respect that kind of a request.

Tom: That's correct. By the way I referenced the Richards Group, but I could've referenced the Martin Agency. That's just another example.

PL: Let's go back quickly to something you said earlier. Are you seeing that clients are using the same process for projects and AOR reviews?

Tom: In too many instances, the process for project reviews is more complicated than is warranted based on the size of the opportunity.

We just did a pilot survey among the 4A's statistics committee members. About a quarter of them will not pitch for a project. They will work on projects as a way to establish both rapport and the ability to start to work together. But they simply will not pitch for the right to work on a project. They just don't think that the economics makes sense.

Some of the evolution of this whole project review thing largely comes out of two elements. First is the growth of digital activities and that digital marketing is primarily a project-driven way of working. So while even big digital agencies like 360i or RGA have very significant relationships with very significant clients, their relationships tend to be a litany of projects, one after another or multiple projects going at the same time rather than an AOR retainer situation. Part of the growth of projects is a function of digital, social, and PR experimentation and first of its kind work being done.

The second element is the Great Recession of 2008 - 2010, when clients simply were not in a mode of wanting to commit anything beyond what was absolutely necessary. So clients began to meter out and authorize activities on a shorter leash. Even as the economy has recovered to whatever degree, it's become a standard pattern.

PL: So what we've seen is a behavioral shift?

Tom: In some instances I'd agree with that, yes.

PL: Do your smaller agencies view projects as an opportunity for them vs. when the majority of pitches were AOR? Does this benefit the smaller more specialized agency?

Tom: Absolutely. If you consider going back 25 or 30 years ago, relationships between the agency and the client tended to be exclusive arrangements in both directions. As clients started to unbundle – everything from unbundling research, to unbundling promotion activities, to unbundling media, and so on – there was also the growth of more specialist firms, whether it be search firms, web development firms, specialists in mobile app development, and so on. Clients now work with far more agencies today than they worked with 25, 30 years ago. And that creates opportunities for specialists. And some of those specialists, quite frankly, can overcome a size deficit by having that deep expertise in a specific niche. It's definitely created opportunities for smaller organizations.

PL: And your agencies are recognizing that trying to be everything to everybody is not necessarily the best business development case?

Tom: Well, there are two heads to that coin. Yes, clients are working with more agencies than ever before. But when you ask the clients what their paramount challenges are, one of the top ones is how they integrate all this stuff. So you will see clients go through a process of expanding the number of agencies, and then from time to time, take a step back and say "This is out of control. We have to rationalize some of this, there are too many inefficiencies of having all these agencies. We can't manage all of this." So the concept of a lead agency is not over by any means.

PL: So how does a smaller agency protect itself when it's time for consolidation?

Tom: Well if a small agency has a deep expertise in an area, they may well survive and actually thrive in a consolidation.

PL: An enlightening interview in this book is with the procurement expert Gerry Preece. One of the most revealing statements he made was that when it comes to compensation negotiations, advertising agencies are like babes being led to the slaughter. How do you help your members learn how to negotiate?

Tom: At most sizeable marketers, procurement has taken over the lead responsibilities for negotiating compensation, and you have to recognize they are trained, skilled negotiators. If you send untrained account people into a negotiation with procurement, the agency is going to get the fudge handed to them.

It should be noted that when procurement says things like "This is it. Take it or leave it.", procurement, most of the time, doesn't have the authority to say that. They don't have the authority to make that decision. But if procurement says, "We'd love to work with you, but unfortunately your costs are too high.", you have to recognize that they're going to tell you that even if you're the lowest cost agency. So there are strategies for negotiating that agencies must develop. Part of the strategy is not to let procurement isolate the agency from the marketing and most senior management of the client.

PL: Well having the CMO involved sounds critical. How can you make that happen? How do you get marketing management into the room?

Tom: Well that's the job for the lead client service director or the head of the agency to make sure that the CMO is not abdicating responsibility. The Great Recession empowered procurement. So CMOs should have evolved to work more collaboratively with their own procurement groups.

PL: So as it often comes down to it, it's about agencies asking CMOs to participate and for agencies to act proactively. How can they get there?

Tom: The 4A's have conducted a number of negotiating skills training programs for our members. One of the negotiating skills trainers we work with is Tim Brenton of the Brenton Group. Tim talks about TDQs: Tough Disturbing Questions. And to your point, you can't negotiate unless you're prepared to ask tough questions. So when the client provides contractor sort of terms and says it's non-negotiable, you have to push back and say everything's negotiable. We don't accept non-negotiation, and who has authorized you to make that declaration? You know, push back at 'em.

PL: Interesting. Pushing back is difficult for some "nice" advertising people.

Tom: It's clearly difficult for an account person who says, "If we lose this business, I don't have a portfolio to work with."

PL: I love the idea of asking Tough Disturbing Questions, that's fantastic, and I think Gerry's earlier point is you have to be able to come back hard. It is important to note that by the time the client has selected you after a three to four month process, they're fully invested in wanting to work with you, and it's incumbent upon agencies to leverage that.

Tom: Yes. And the fact that they selected you is an indication that whatever it is that you presented, whatever it is that your process is and so on, that's what they want. The decision is almost never made on money. In survey work we've done, money doesn't even crack the top five or six decision-making criteria.

PL: Here is my last question: What is the one piece of advice that you'd give agencies to help them win?

Tom: Pitch less.

My advice is that agencies have to ruthlessly screen opportunities, and stop ambulance chasing. And in point of fact, my recommendation is that agencies make a conscious, strategic decision to reduce their traditional pitch activity by twenty percent.

They should take that money and resource and invest it in developing their own intellectual property that the agency owns and monetizes. And go to market with that intellectual property, license the things that you develop to clients, and develop control of your own intellectual property. If you did that over a three, four or five year period, it would be a significant war chest of investment, and you would have a significantly different model of business development that is much more within the agency's own control, particularly the pricing of that intellectual property.

PL: Do you have an example of an agency that is building an intellectual property treasure chest?

Tom: Unfortunately no. No, I am not aware of any agency that has specifically adopted the 20% formula. That being said, there are an increasing number of agency experiments with agencies adopting their own I.P.

For example:

Schafer Carter Condon developed a beer brand, which they then sold to a beverage company.

Digital agencies like T3 and Sarkissian have independently developed patented software service platforms, which they license to marketers.

Anomaly has developed multiple products including a cosmetics line.

Media agencies have independently invested in software, data and analytics models which are the foundation of agency owned and controlled trading desks.

Agencies are investing sweat equity in the developing of social platforms, apps, and content which they are endeavoring to monetize across multiple platforms.

This function requires a multi-year commitment: it's not going to happen overnight. The industry has to start to use some of its own creativity and technical know-how when developing its own products and services. Because if you develop your own intellectual property, it stops being a procurement discussion. It's not "How many hours did you put into this?" It's not "What do you pay your people, what's your profit margin, what's your overhead rate?" And the only way out of that nonsense is to be able to control the intellectual property.

––––––––

Sitting On Both Sides of The Table

Over the years, I've spoken with a couple of agency executives that made the jump to the agency search consultant side of the table. It was interesting to hear their first impressions as pitch voyeurs on how agencies present. It is a great perspective since agency people rarely get to look at their industry from the other side of the table.

INTERVIEW
Tony Mikes: Managing Director, Second Wind Network

Tony Mikes is the Founder and Managing Director of the Second Wind Network which has 800 small to mid-sized agency members.

Tony has been consulting with and advising advertising agencies and business concerns for almost 20 years. He provides members and clients with "old school" agency wisdom, combined with cutting-edge strategies. Before starting Second Wind, he was President of Pennsylvania's Mikes & Reese Advertising from 1972 to 1988.

My agency Citrus was a member of Second Wind, and Tony was one of our advisors.

PL: You were on the client side of the agency selection table recently. How did that go?

Tony: I spent my entire working life in the advertising agency business. At mid-career, I found myself founding the agency network Second Wind. It is my second life. After having spent 26 years running the network, I got a call from an ex-agency member from San Diego. He had gone on to a major zoo in San Diego and then on to the National Aquarium in Baltimore. He was not happy with his agency, didn't know a lot about Baltimore or East Coast agencies, and asked if I would serve as the consultant to the Aquarium to help them choose an agency. This was a unique position for me. In all the years I've been in the business, I have never ever been on the other side of the table.

PL: And what was the Aquarium looking for in an agency? What was the master brief?

Tony: Well the master brief was essentially a search for a traditional media buying and creative agency. The client also had existing relationships with PR and digital agencies. The bulk of the budget, around 2 million dollars, was going to the agency that would win the business.

PL: What process did you use to build an initial long list? How long was it?

Tony: Because the Aquarium is a funded organization, a 501(c)(3), the search was a bit more public than usual. So the list was long, because everybody in management threw somebody into the hopper, and there were absolutely no criteria set for management's recommendations. On top of that, we had another list that was built using marketing objectives. This list was built on geography, specialty, expertise, and former personal working experience. So there were two long lists that combined ended up being about 50 agencies.

PL: 50, wow. So 50 agencies were sent an RFP. Did you help craft the RFP?

Tony: I did. I had plenty of them on file at the network, and that was one of the reasons the client wanted to use me. Most of the agencies did not respond to the RFP.

PL: Interesting. Why would an agency decline? It's not like they had a whale or porpoise client conflict.

Tony: Well, some declined because they were busy. One particular agency that I liked declined because they just had too many things to do, and then a number of agencies from around Baltimore declined because they had felt that the client was tough. At the end, 20 agencies responded.

PL: And your goal was to reduce that initial 20 to how many agencies?

Tony: I would've wanted three, but it became six.

PL: Did you see a large difference in how agencies responded to the RFP?

Tony: Yes. Although I will say that of the 20 that submitted, probably 15 put together very acceptable written proposals. In answering the questions, in sticking to the topic, in putting their agency's credentials forward, in answering the couple of spec questions that we asked - we didn't ask for spec work but we asked for some spec thinking. But the other 5 kinda just threw stuff together like it was printed off of the printer; no binding, paper clips at the top – they were pretty easy to spot, and they really easy to turn away.

PL: Why do you think an agency can wind up delivering such a half-assed response?

Tony: I don't think they know any better.

PL: Interesting and somewhat sad, right?

Tony: My educated guess is that they just don't know what they don't know. Having been involved with over 800 agencies, I am not surprised at the wide range of agency knowledge.

PL: What were your criteria for choosing the short list?

Tony: We had a rating system. I helped the client build a scorecard. Everybody individually scored these agencies, and then we met and talked about each agency and their scores. This process yielded the final 6.

PL: How many people were on the selection committee?

Tony: There were two consultants: a woman from Baltimore who was really mostly concerned with the image of the Aquarium and me as the agency pro and then an additional six people from the aquarium staff, so eight in total.

PL: How did you make a final selection?

Tony: We wanted to have a face-to-face presentation. The RFP was designed to see if the agencies could follow instructions, fulfill the capabilities, and look like they had enough gravitas to manage the 2 million dollar budget.

PL: How long did you give each agency to present?

Tony: An hour.

PL: Did you give them specific questions, or did you leave it up to them at that point?

Tony: There was another step in between the RFP and the presentation. Once we chose the 6, we notified them and told them they could send us questions. There were a couple weeks where people were just trying to get themselves prepared. But we did not give them anything specific to present. In fact, I thought from my experience, we would allow them to have some room so we could see what their in-person presentations were like.

PL: Did you find that all of the agencies used that period where they could ask you questions as a branding tool for themselves? Did they use this time as a pre-sales opportunity?

Tony: I think that certainly four of the six were able to do a little pre-selling.

PL: It's just such a great opportunity to demonstrate insights and frankly, show passion.

Tony: Right. And I think passion was important for this thing.

PL: So they came into, I'm assuming, a conference room at the Aquarium – was that the physical setup?

Tony: No, I advised the client to have the agencies go to a third-party location with one door in and one door out. I was fairly adamant about giving the agencies a fair shot and that the agencies would not see each other before or after. I always thought that was very inconvenient to meet up with the next presenter.

PL: Me too, it is bit awkward. In the presentations, were there clearly things that worked and things that didn't?

Tony: Well, the first presentation was terrible because none of the rules, in my mind, were followed. They just started, and there was just no logic to what they were doing to pass the ball from one to another. They didn't start strong, they didn't close strong.

Only the sixth agency was killer.

PL: And how did they kill it? What did they do right?

Tony: They were exuberant, for one thing.

PL: And how many people were there on that team?

Tony: Four people. They stage-managed and asked us if they could come in the night before to change the setup to be in schoolroom style rather than conference style. We all felt obligated to oblige. So the tables had already been reset by them the night before the presentation so they could make their way through the room. They had asked specifically who would attend, and they had asked all the proper questions about the computer connections and projectors. They were absolutely ready for the dance.

PL: So to be clear, of the six agencies, how many wanted to know who from the client would be in the room?

Tony: Nobody else.

PL: That's... crazy.

Tony: Yeah, I mean, I think that that's a sin, maybe not mortal, but that's certainly a sin. But nobody asked.

PL: Well that's incredibly surprising considering the importance of making interpersonal connections. What else did the smart agency do that stood out?

Tony: There was a pitch leader, and he occupied the podium. The other three presenters sat on director's chairs. The leader moderated the whole session. So anything that needed to be stopped or moved or changed or accelerated or decelerated – the leader had control. The leader read the room and controlled the flow.

PL: Did you have a sense that they were well rehearsed?

Tony: Yes. They certainly had rehearsed a lot. They started with a bang – without introductions. Dark room. Killer video. Which ended in a... here we are.

The video lasted about a couple minutes. It was really great.

PL: Was the video about them or about the client?

Tony: No, no. It was about something the Aquarium had said to every agency but not every agency picked up. *"We are not heavily funded by the United States government. We depend upon donations, mostly on admissions. Having said that, we're not an attraction. We are very mission-driven. And the mission is sustainability of ocean life."* So this agency started with a sustainability of ocean life video. It was a home run right at the beginning. You could see the Aquarium director get up and just kinda fidget around in his chair a little bit because an agency finally had stopped talking about themselves first. The video talked about the Aquarium's mission and the vision, which was more about sustainability than being an attraction.

When that video ended, I believed they had won.

They had done their homework, they had listened carefully to what the client had to say, and they had brought that back to the agency and finessed it in a way that only smart agencies can do.

Other than that video, they did not use PowerPoint. The agency director believed that PowerPoint is too linear and not personal enough. Everything they did was on boards, and the boards were passed around. So consequently, when they were passing the boards around, they were in the middle of everybody because they had reset the room to schoolroom style. They could go past us, could kinda touch us on the sleeve, could joke with us just a bit, et cetera, et cetera, et cetera. Cool idea.

PL: What kind of boards did they use?

Tony: Typical size. They must've been 22" by 28".

PL: It sounds like they made the pitch an intimate experience.

Tony: It was intimate, yes. Very quickly intimate, because they had begun to circulate.

The key point is to try to set the room up the way you want, and set it up for intimacy – so that you can roam around. Also, you know there's certainly nothing wrong with the intimacy of boards.

PL: Did all the other agencies present using some form of PowerPoint?

Tony: Yes. Now some did have some boards that were passed around, but by and large, every other presentation was largely, profoundly, PowerPoint driven.

PL: And did the other agencies use video in any way? Customized video?

Tony: They did use customized video. Although, it was more of a "here's us" than a "here's your sustainability thing". The agency videos were "here's who we are."

PL: So let me get this straight: some of the agencies showed you a video of themselves. Of what? Here's our agency furniture?

Tony: Yeah. And the fact that we have a cool lobby, and we serve beer at

4 o'clock on Fridays. Fuck that, everybody does that. Excuse my French.

PL: It sounds to me like this agency made a three-part sandwich. Intimacy plus insights plus chemistry. Am I nailing that?

Tony: Well I would add surprise onto that. The dark room and the sustainability video were a surprise. We did not expect it.

PL: So they figured out the passion inherent in the client's mission.

Tony: They did. This agency hit my big three rules: these guys know what they're talking about, and I believe they can help us, and I like 'em. And wow look what they just did.

PL: Was it clear to the group that there was a winner?

Tony: Yes.

PL: Do you think that agency knew that they had won it when they walked out of the room?

Tony: I don't know if they knew. But we knew. The committee knew. I now believe that in most pitches the winner is known as soon as the last presenter presents. You know it. In other words, we didn't have to go around and add all these crazy scorecards. We looked at each other and said "well, gosh, does everybody kinda feel the way I feel?" We followed the process, but we all knew the outcome. We still used the scorecards but it was more about keeping to our agreed process.

PL: Do you think an agency's position in the rotation mattered? Is it better to be first or last?

Tony: I don't know that, and that's the question a lot of people ask. All I can say is I'd rather not be in the middle.

PL: So it's like the middle child complex.

Tony: Yeah it's the middle child complex. First you get a chance to really kinda knock 'em off their feet, and then people have to kinda live up to you at that point. But last agency gets the chance to close strong. However, they risk that the client is tired as hell because they've just gone through two days of presentations. That's three agencies a day. And so they're really, really tired. But last still outweighs being in the middle.

PL: And how long before the presentation did the agency know what position they were in?

Tony: They knew it when we formally wrote them and told them when the presentations would take place.

PL: Knowing that, a savvy agency would be saying to themselves: okay, this client is going to be tired, they've just heard a whole bunch of agencies say the same thing over and over again, we better lead with a good right hook.

Tony: Yeah, I think that's exactly it.

PL: I have to admit I'm surprised that agencies are always making the kinds of mistakes that you would think a grown-up marketing communications company would not make. That's very hard to understand.

Tony: I never cease to be amazed at what agencies stumble on. Not just in the business of pitching. But in everyday agency life. But, that's another story.

There were some other things that worked: after this great opening and because of the room, the agency kept their team involved. Also, they stated the marketing problem and solved it. That's a practical piece of advice - solve the problem. Actually say that you've solved it.

PL: So let me understand. When the agency showed their thinking, it was their best strategic guess at how they were going to help the client.

Tony: Yeah, they guessed. I think a lot of agencies would be shy to say "well this is just speculation", but listen, the whole damn thing is speculation. So you might as well spec the results.

PL: Got it.

Tony: Another thing that came up was that since this was a media account, the winner was very adamant about showing their media capabilities: the number of markets they were in, the capabilities they had with software, the backgrounds of their media staff, even though there was no media person on site with them. And I didn't know why. They did tell me after the fact that their media director was just an intellectual guru and not a great presenter.

PL: Well, I always recommend that agencies don't bring poor presenters.

Tony: That's right. Don't bring poor presenters.

And I think it's fantastic that the agency was upfront about their media director and said she's brilliant. What a brain. A brainiac. But she's a nerd and doesn't do well in front of people, in a presentation. But you'll love working with her.

Get this, she wrote the client a personal note that was read in the meeting.

PL: Smart. I've never heard of this one.

Tony: They closed strong by asking for the business, which goes back all the way to a classic sales technique – ask for the order.

To recap: they had a positive attitude, they got into their ideas rather quickly, they made the experience interactive, they listened and looked for buying signs, and they knew who we were before they got into the room. Sounds basic, right? But, it clearly isn't.

PL: I mean, you know that you don't have to do everything that the sales gurus tell you. But asking for the order is a very good move.

Tony: Yes. Asking for the order is a good thing.

PL: A great move. And how did the agencies follow up after presentations?

Tony: Several didn't say a word. Others were very pesky. But the Aquarium director was very good at writing emails that assured the agencies that the process was moving forward. We did not solicit any more topics from them after the presentations.

PL: Did every agency have a leave behind?

Tony: No. Not even the winning agency.

PL: Did anyone do a particularly good job with a leave behind?

Tony: Well, there were some stupid jobs. One agency asked us at the end to get together with them and put together a puzzle that they had made, that eventually said "well, give us the business."

PL: And they sent that. They sent that after the meeting?

Tony: No, no they actually invited people to put it together with them right there in the room. I didn't think it was a bad approach. I just thought it was too cute.

PL: Would a leave behind have helped any of the agencies score more points? Like they say in the play, Glengarry Glen Ross… "always be selling."

Tony: Probably. But it should really be in the form of something that is memorable. Not just "Here's the brochure of our presentation." I think four of the six directed people to a landing page that they had built for questions and further investigations, which I thought was a good idea.

PL: **We are at the end and this has been enlightening. Bear with me, a final, final question: what was the biggest mistake an agency made.**

Tony: One agency did nothing but show their previous work. That's all they did.

PL: **So the ultimate sin, the cardinal sin, is to talk about yourself and not the client. And one of your finalists actually did that?**

Tony: Yes. And with good reason. Because they had premium work. The work was so funny, so much on target, so nicely done, that the agency leader said "we don't have anything to show you but what we've done for other folks."

And that was the strategy. Unfortunately, it didn't work, and they lost the pitch during their presentation. We needed more than faith to go on.

———

INTERVIEW
Michael Mosynski, CEO, LONDON Advertising

Michael Mosynski is CEO of LONDON Advertising. He launched the agency five years ago as a global agency built for today's marketplace. The agency's clients include Boots No7, Mandarin Oriental Hotel Group, Ketel One, W&O Travel, and Wegwood.

Prior to starting LONDON, Michael was the CEO of M&C Saatchi Hong Kong, Middle East, and London's IS. Prior to joining M&C Saatchi, he held a range of senior positions at Saatchi & Saatchi Advertising Worldwide.

PL: **LONDON Advertising is positioned as an international, yet very nimble one-office agency that that delivers "*One Brilliant Idea that can work in any media, anywhere in the world.*" Why does this positioning generate interest from multinational clients?**

Michael: Clients tend to see their communication challenges as highly complex. When these need to be addressed across different markets, languages, and cultures, these challenges are magnified in their minds to the power of 10.

LONDON's promise to develop "One Brilliant Idea" that works everywhere is 'Marketing Nirvana', although sometimes clients think it is too good to be true, so then our challenge is to prove it is possible.

We do that by showing numerous case studies where we have done it for a diverse range of businesses. It is the simplicity we bring that is so appealing to clients.

We can also point to the very clear benefits of achieving simplicity as we can prove it delivers the highest possible ROI for our clients in their sector.

PL: You won the global Boots No7 account. How did an agency with only one office in London get the attention of such a large client with international needs?

Michael: Although as a recent start-up we are not well known in the client community (the truth is few agencies are), our positioning was something we had successfully communicated to the industry pitch consultants.

I was in my car taking my kids to the country for the start of the summer holidays when I got a call from Suki Thompson who runs the UK's leading agency search consultancy, The Oystercatchers.

Suki asked if LONDON had any experience in women's beauty products, launching brands in Finland, and developing social media–led campaigns.

As we had none of the requisite experience, I of course replied "yes" and then asked if I could call her back once I had reached my destination.

Whilst driving for the next hour, I racked my brain and remembered that a very experienced strategic planner we work with regularly had previously worked at P&G where she led the global relaunch of Oil of Ulay. I called her and checked if she was free to work with us on this pitch and enquired if, on the off-chance, she also had any experience of working in Finland. As it turned out, she had just come back from Helsinki where she had conducted a series of focus groups to help an international insurance company develop its entry strategy for the market.

So I rang back Suki, who on the basis of this experience, put us on the Boots list.

PL: What was the pitch scenario? Did it start with an RFP, and did you get to meet the client ahead of the pitch?

Michael: We were sent an outline brief of the challenge ahead of a credentials/chemistry meeting with the client which, in the too oft-used phrase used in new business, 'went well'. And this time it actually had.

As our planner had a unique range of experience as a market researcher, marketing client, agency strategic planner, and management consultant at McKinsey, we asked if she could have a follow up meeting with the Brand Manager.

This enabled us to deepen our relationship and make sure the client understood the level of experience we could apply to their brief as well as get a better understanding of what they were looking for. This was invaluable on both counts.

One of the advantages of our business model is we can bring in the right resource at a very senior level for a client based on their needs rather than who happens to be in the agency.

The strategic planner's daily rate is three times that of a typical agency planner, but she is worth every penny. Our model also means that the client benefits from that experience and is not paying the agency to learn at their expense. And from an agency perspective, it means we get to the right solution, first time, more often than other agencies. This saves us, and the client, time and money.

PL: What was the pitch for?

Michael: The pitch was to test market the launch of Alliance Boots No7 Brand for the first time as a stand-alone FMCG product.

Previously No7 had only been sold in markets that had a Boots retail presence. As Alliance Boots was owned by a VC, it was strategically important for them to demonstrate that the company had assets it could grow outside of opening more retail stores in the UK.

PL: Where were the other agencies you pitched against?

Michael: At the outset, the client was unsure if they needed a Finnish or a UK-based agency. They felt the former could provide more local insight, but the latter could create a campaign idea that could then be rolled-out to other markets.

Having got under the skin of the client's requirements, we worked out that what we needed was local insight into the attitudes of Finnish women and the beauty market, integrated communications planning advice, and an in-depth knowledge of Finnish social media.

As we were not a 'JWT Worldwide', we did not have to use 'JWT Helsinki' and were therefore free to evaluate the best candidate from five specific Finns we identified through our talent network. We selected the person who best met our criteria, and he was brilliant.

Our approach gave the client the best of both world's and so they ultimately felt comfortable working with LONDON – an agency in London.

PL: What worked in your pitch?

Michael: Without telling the client, we paid for our Finnish comms planner/ social media guru to fly to London to work with us on our pitch. As we had developed it in partnership, it felt very natural and a good fit when we presented it.

How many times does a client attend an international pitch with a network agency to see the team members introducing themselves and handing over interagency business cards to each other in front of the client?

The campaign we developed for Finland was very innovative and resulted in the highest ad recall of any ad in Finland despite having a tiny budget. Based on this success, we were appointed agency of record for the No7 Brand globally, and our work has since run on every continent.

PL: Was the pitch run by the client or the pitch consultant? If a consultant is involved, do you change the way you work?

Michael: This pitch was kicked off by a consultant but not run by them.

We tend to work in the same way in any case to get to the right answer.

Some consultants are, to be frank, better than others, and you have to understand they also have an agenda – to give the client a range of campaigns that cover different aspects of the brief, so one must be careful not to always take their feedback at face value.

PL: Did it make you nervous to go up against network agencies? Some small agencies might think that they are just a spoiler with no chance of winning. Why did you think LONDON had a chance of winning this account?

Michael: We relish big challenges, so feeling nervous is not a sensation we are familiar with.

There is the point though to only enter pitches when you have a reasonable chance of winning them.

I would admit in hindsight, we have too often agreed to participate in pitches where the client would not have considered in a million years a non-network agency. However this issue is usually resolved at the creds or chemistry stages.

I believe it is quite legitimate for a consultant to offer the client a choice of our approach to see if the client would consider a new way to developing global campaigns. So whilst we don't win them all, it is an advantage to get on pitch lists most agencies could only dream about, by being positioned as the wild card.

When my business partner, Alan Jarvie, and I set up M&C Saatchi in Hong Kong, we were asked to pitch for HSBC across Asia in our first year when we only had six people. The other four agencies were all established network agencies with over 250 staff. The HK ad industry thought we had no chance going after such an established client.

We were known by HSBC as "the wild card that came up trumps", and when our win was announced, it made it onto the front page of *The Times* 8,000 miles away and led to a 15 minute feature about our small agency that ran on CNBC globally.

Our *schadenfreude* in HK was also rather delightful.

Following our appointment, we ended up recommending that the bank rebrand globally under the HSBC name, and we made their first global TV campaign which was one of the biggest achievements of our careers. Not bad for a small agency.

I was once told that the failure of most new companies is that they think 'too small' so we have never let size be an issue.

When we wanted to grow our digital capability at LONDON, we set up our own digital talent competition with a £100,000 prize and set ourselves the goal of getting the British Prime Minister, David Cameron, to launch it. He kindly obliged to do so from Downing Street.

PL: Network agencies make a very big deal about the geographic breadth of their network and its global reach. Do you think that having an office in every country is a 1980's concept that isn't as valuable in 2014?

Michael: In the past, to develop a global campaign, clients needed a global network agency, so the fact we can do this today from one office is appealing to clients who don't need 'boots on the ground' in '67 countries'. (Do you remember when every agency creds started with a slide showing a map of the world and the line *'We are everywhere you are?'*)

We set up LONDON to be a global agency from day one and were able to do so with a blank sheet of paper. As all the agency networks were created before the advent of the Internet, they have a legacy infrastructure they can't change to compete with our proposition.

We applied the benefits of the internet to how we organize the back-end processes of creating and delivering global campaigns. We have a virtual network of strategic planners and local language copywriters covering over 150 markets. And of course today, all the work can be supplied digitally, so you no longer need an office in Jakarta to create and supply an ad to a local paper – or a Facebook campaign in Helsinki.

Our model is best demonstrated by our pitch for the campaign to support Fox International's largest global launch of a new show, "The Walking Dead." We had to pitch against agencies in the US, Brazil, South Africa, and Italy. Our winning idea, 'Stay in', ran in 135 markets in 36 countries.

PL: Do you have another example that shows your model working for a client?

Michael: Last year we were approached by the CEO of the legacy luxury Swiss watch brand, H. Moser. Currently H. Moser is a relatively small brand but one with big ambitions to grow 500% in next five years.

The agency task was to define the brand and execute it across all communications. We were able to convince the client that rather than holding a competitive pitch, we alone would do the work, and if they liked what we developed, we would get the business.

The client agreed, and we treated it internally as a competitive pitch, generating initially 19 different campaigns, which we condensed down to 5 strategic/creative areas and presented these to the client in a 'tissue session'.

From their feedback, we developed a final recommendation and prepared a full-on pitch that made the argument that to do justice to their ambition, they needed to create a brand asset that differentiated them in the watch market and would enable them to cut-through a category where every ad features a large photograph of a watch showing the hands at '10 to 2'.

We flipped the fact there were few H. Moser watches into a positive with our One Brilliant Idea of 'Very Rare'. The launch ad summarized the campaign:

"H. Moser watches. So rare they don't even appear in H. Moser watch advertisements."

The client loved the idea and appointed us on the basis of our 'one agency pitch'.

The campaign has since run in English, Cantonese, Mandarin, Japanese, Russian, Arabic, French, German and Italian. And we have integrated 'Very Rare' into their website, videos, brochures, online, events, merchandise, sponsorships, endorsements, trade campaign, and point-of-sale.

PL: How can smaller agencies compete with network agencies?

Michael: *"Know thyself and to thine own self be true."*

Don't try to compensate for perceived weaknesses, but play to your strengths and flip the decision-making process. Turn your weakness into an advantage – whether that is as a specialist, by being more nimble, or whatever.

PL: Do you have a secret sauce that you can share?

Michael: We have a clear, unique positioning combined with unparalleled international experience that is difficult to replicate. My creative partner and I have worked together for 21 years having set up and run businesses for the Saatchis in London, Hong Kong, New York, and The Middle East.

We can point to the fact that despite all the challenges of the pitch process, the work we have presented in pitches for all our major clients has actually run – including the 'He's a Fan' campaign for Mandarin Oriental which is now entering its 15th year unchanged – apart from three new celebrities each year who, unusually, we do not pay to take part.

PL: Do you have a pitch story that still enters your nightmares?

Michael: We were shortlisted for a very significant pitch where the chemistry meeting went brilliantly based on some great insight into the audience that the marketing team loved. We went to the next meeting where we met the CEO with whom we shared our 'brilliant' thinking. His reply was that the part of the client brief which inspired our thinking was a load of 'tosh' and that by implication, we were idiots for swallowing it. He then proceeded to provide a detailed picture portrait about who the real audience was.

As he was the CEO, we took him to be the key decision-maker, and whilst our final presentation knocked the ball out of the park with him, we lost the pitch. We had not met the owner until the day of the pitch, and he agreed with the marketing team, not the CEO.

The lessons from this were three-fold:

1. Make sure you really understand who are the decision-makers and what influences them

2. Take your own medicine (see the earlier mention of, "…*to thine own self be true*")

3. Stick to your principles and don't be swayed by the size of the prize (easier to say…)

Truth be told, we *had* agreed with the marketing team, but having lost other pitches for doing what *we* believed was the right thing, we did not want to let this 'biggy' get away. Doh!

PL: My discussions with clients, search consultants, and agency leaders continuously point to the importance of client-agency "chemistry" in agency selection. Do you have any techniques that you use to try to build chemistry?

Michael: As above (again), my advice is "…*to thine own self be true*."

In fact, have that message tattooed in reverse on your forehead so you see it in the mirror every morning before heading off to the office.

It is like applying for a job or going on a date – don't act out what you think the client wants you to be, otherwise you will end up in an unhappy relationship.

The reason chemistry is so important is that:

a. people buy from people
b. people buy emotionally and then justify their decision rationally

My key tip for pitching is something I read recently that is so obvious that perhaps it is forgotten too easily. When preparing any presentation, don't start with what you want to communicate – whether it is your agency proposition or your client's objectives etc. Plan every presentation by thinking about the audience in the room. Know them and make sure you engage with them as people.

And that means winning their hearts first – but don't forget to give them the reasons that they can tell their boss why they appointed you.

PL: In your experience, are their any glaring pitch mistakes that agency's make?

Michael: Typos.

(See 'their' above – sorry Peter, but yours was a gift to make my point, so please don't change it in the final galleys!)

The reason why typos are so glaring, is apart from impacting on the client's confidence in your attention to detail (*"gosh if they can't get it right in their pitch to us will they run typos in our ads?"*) is that the reader then ignores the point you were attempting to make as all they see is the error.

On a more strategic level, the biggest mistake that agencies make in pitches is falling into the trap of giving away our product for free and then attempting to get paid by our inefficiency in producing bits of cardboard.

Clients' approach to remuneration tends to discourage agencies who have small teams who can do the work quickly and efficiently. At LONDON we try to get round this by being entrepreneurial in how we work with clients by having both a performance-related pay element and a licensing deal to our IP that guarantees us a minimum level of income for developing their long-term One Brilliant Idea irrespective of how much cardboard manipulation we carry out.

But to be frank, it is hard as we are still operating in a competitive context where our agency peers have already pulled their pants down whilst simultaneously raising the white flag.

The good news is there is clearly a great future in writing books advising the rest of the advertising industry on what to do…

––––––––

The Contrarian View

Need more advice? In this case it's more super honest, absolutely no bull shit advice from the leading honest, no bull shit voice in the world of advertising.

Bob Hoffman is an author, speaker, and partner in Type A Group, LLC, a company that consults with marketers, advertisers, and media.

He is author of *101 Contrarian Ideas About Advertising* which is Amazon's #1 selling advertising book, *The Ad Contrarian* and *The Ad Contrarian* blog, which was named one of the world's most influential advertising and marketing blogs by Business Insider.

Bob founded and was Chairman / CEO of Hoffman/Lewis Advertising, one of the West's largest independent advertising agencies. Bob was named "Ad Person of the Year" in 2012 by the San Francisco Advertising Club.

By the way, this is how a contrarian thinks about the advertising industry.

"Nobody really knows what "creativity" is. Every year thousands of people take a pilgrimage to find out. This involves flying to Cannes, snorting cocaine, and having sex with smokers."

I asked Bob for his thoughts on new business:

1. **You can't be everyone's girlfriend:** Do not pitch every stupid thing that comes along. Don't try to fit yourself into every box. Not everyone is going to love you, and not everyone is going to buy your story. Pick your spots.

2. **Do what you tell your clients to do.** The first thing we tell our clients is that they have to differentiate themselves. It is the *one thing* agencies never do. They all sound the same, look the same, and smell the same. Decide who you are and how you are different and better. If you can't do that, hire Peter and let him do it for you.

3. **Be clear on your objective at each stage.** This is really important. A new business pitch is a 3 or 4 step process. At each stage your one and

only objective should be to get to the next stage. You will not win the account at the first stage. At the beginning stages, clients are not looking to hire an agency, they are looking for reasons to eliminate agencies. Give them reasons why they should continue talking to you, and don't give them reasons to eliminate you.

4. **Make the presentation you want to make, not the one you're asked to make.** For the final pitch, most of the time clients and search consultants provide you with outlines of the presentation they want to see. Throw it away and make the presentation you want to make. Remember, you have one shot only.

5. **Only let the good presenters talk.** There are brilliant people who are lousy presenters and dumb-ass bozos who are great presenters. Only let the good presenters present.

6. **Have a strategy and stick to it.** The final presentation should have a theme, and every section of the presentation should spin off that theme and point to a conclusion where the strategy is clearly and creatively defined.

7. **By the way, the best new business program is a good reputation.** Duh.

CHAPTER **7**

THE FRONTLINES

Sixteen Agency Search Consultants On "The Single Worst Presentation Mistakes"

Just because I was in the mood to highlight even more agency mistakes, I asked sixteen of the world's leading agency search consultants for their answers to the question, "What are the worst pitch mistakes agencies make?"

These opinions come from consultants that have sat through thousands of agency pitches. After reading their comments, imagine the eye rolling that they must do when many of us are presenting our truly brilliant ideas and work.

Again, my goal is to point out what *not* to do. Hidden between the lines of these answers is what *to* do to help you win.

Vasily Ananin: Agency Assessments International, Russia

Here are my thoughts on the topic of your question:

To present, the people in the pitch should have the best presentation skills throughout the agency.

Presenters should be able to answer any client questions without the help of colleagues.

If you want to win the pitch, it is better that the presentation is conducted by the GM of the advertising agency.

One of the biggest mistakes during the pitch is that the agency offers services that they can't knowingly perform. I mean that the agency, during the tender, promises to customers something that they obviously can't deliver (they are bluffing). This behavior has a very negative impact on the reputation of the agency.

Laura Bajkowski: Principle, Bajkowski+Partners, New York

Talking at the client prospect rather than engaging them in the pitch experience.

This has run the gamut from going around the table and introducing themselves, yet totally skipping the client attendees, to droning on about how great their case studies are, but never connecting the dots back to this client's business.

Ten minutes of agency droning on about anything other than the client's business feels like an eternity to the client. Get to points quickly, connect everything back to client's business, and get the client talking too. And don't forget to read the room – if you're savvy, you can tell when you're losing them.

Cramming everything into the final pitch presentation. We work with clients to keep the assignments focused, but there are always other basic details that are best highlighted in a graphic or left for the pitch book. So agencies cram a lot of content in and rehearse it to death to determine how much faster they need to talk, rather than what can go in the pitch book. And they seem to overlook how to draw the clients into the process.

Clients love info-graphics, and it's a great way to communicate and crystalize a lot of complex content – don't know why more agencies don't do this or something more visual more often.

Paul Bainsfair: Director General, Institute of Practitioners in Advertising (IPA), UK

Virtually every agency goes on for far too long about itself and its team.

Cut to the chase. Talk about how the brief has been solved, and get to the answer quickly. The clients will thank you for it, and they will decide if they want to work with you based on how they FEEL about you, not what you tell them about yourselves.

Robin Boehler: Partner, Mercer Island Group, Washington

The worst presentation mistake that agencies make is to focus on the wrong things.

The wrong things are typically:

- Themselves: They focus on their agency and their capabilities
- Marketing tactics: They focus on the tactics they love
- Topics they find interesting: They focus on a topic that they personally find compelling

What's the right thing to focus on? That's simple:

Agencies should focus on the core business issues as defined by the prospect.

Business Issues can be core strategic items like revenue, market share, profitability, growth, penetration, loyalty, etc. Business Issues are rarely tactical – tactics are part of a solution. Tactics, without a Business Issue foundation, are a cost center. No one wants to increase their costs. No one, in fact, wants to "buy" advertising, or media, or digital, or public relations. Rather, prospects are interested in solving their Business Issues.

Smart agencies bond with prospects around their problem – their business issue – not the agency solution.

Pete Bogda: ABA Consulting, Inc., Texas

The common/worst mistakes that agencies make is not starting with the folks who will be on the client team, but load the room with agency top brass and/or stars. When we come back and see the B,C or D team assigned to present the Speculative Assignment, the client becomes confused/upset that they changed so dramatically from the initial pitch.

Lisa Colantuono: Co-President, AAR Partners, New York

Top pitching tip: Agencies need to prove to their prospects that they believe in their mission, vision, and beliefs, not just in the product they're selling. How? By LISTENING! Listening is a lost art. Agencies need to listen twice as much as they speak and understand the prospective client's deepest concerns (especially those that can't be verbalized). When you listen you remove yourself from the issue and hear the other party's strength. Their strength plus agencies' innovations will yield powerful business solutions... which begins with listening carefully!

Peter Cowie: Founding Partner, Oystercatchers, UK

"Don't take too many drugs."

Angus Crowther: Partner, Oystercatchers, UK

The single biggest mistake that agencies make is that they are still desperate to talk about themselves, but the best ones talk about the client from the off.

Joanne Davis: President,
Joanne Davis Consulting, Inc., New York

Single biggest mistake is forgetting the client's brief. So often client (or consultant) sends agencies a brief. Agencies re-write it and build their presentation around the agency's re-written brief. And they forget to go back to read the client's brief.

Mike Drexler: Co-Founder and Managing Director,
Drexler/Fajen Partners, New York

In my opinion, the worst mistake agencies make when presenting is concentrating the pitch on their overall capabilities and not enough on the client's specific business goals and objectives.

Jerry Gibbons: Principle, A-Team Advisors, California

I am not going to give you an exact answer to your question. But I am going to give you one mistake that agencies make that is very common, and while it may not be the "killer" error, it is one that does a great deal in failing to communicate that the agency is a well oiled team that has respect for each other, likes each other, finds their team members interesting and believes that they are lucky to be part of that team.

That mistake is the failure of the pitch team members to really listen to their team members talk and react to what they are saying – nodding, laughing, giving "yeahs" and generally paying attention and responding as if it was the first time they heard it. When the agency's pitch team is listening and responding to what their colleagues are saying, it encourages the client to do the same, and it makes the client want to be part of the interesting dialogue that is going on and to be part of that team.

Debbie Morrison: Director of Consultancy and Best Practice, ISBA, thegoodpitch.com, UK

In terms of things agencies do wrong in pitch presentations, the biggest howler I have come across which instantly alienates the client, is disharmony in the agency pitch team!

Either the session is dominated by one senior person and no other agency team members 'dare' or are given the chance to input. Or there have been times I've experienced in pitches when there has been obvious hostility between agency team members resulting in open warfare during the pitch presentation! Highly off putting and results in an instant de-listing in most cases!

Dan Pearlman: CEO/Managing Partner, Bob Wolf Partners/TPG, California

In answer to your question:

Most agencies don't pay enough attention to the chemistry and culture aspects of their pitch. Where do the philosophies and values of their firm align with those of the client? Are your people communicating well and easily with each other in the pitch? How are your folks attired vs. those on the client side? Do they talk numbers and you talk general concepts? Are they all business and you're all smiley? Be careful of glaring disconnects.

Finally, be careful what you wish for...the client may not be right for you to deliver superior work.

Stuart Pocock: Managing Partner, Roth Observatory, UK

Tricky question – there are lots of mistakes they can make – but a key one is not fully understanding the Client's business issues and how the work they are proposing will impact them.

Brian Sparks, Managing Director: Agency Assessments International, UK and Ireland

Agencies spend far too much time talking about themselves and not enough time addressing the problems of the client. Clients want to hear solutions to their problems, not how great the agency thinks it is. Best advice to agencies – focus on the client, demonstrate real understanding of their issues, unearth commercial as well as consumer insight, keep it simple, and make it memorable!

Joan Weinberg: Agency Select, Hong Kong

In 15 years I've sat in on hundreds of pitch calls. The agencies forget this one maxim: It's like going on a first date.

It all starts before the pitch but here goes, my top four pitch problems.

1. Agencies that spend more than 3 minutes talking about their agency

2. Agencies that don't have someone present strictly to take notes

3. Agencies that don't have a sense of humor

4. Agencies that stick to a script

David Wethey: Chairman, Agency Assessments International, UK

Hard to pick just one reason when I am drawing on AAI's 26 years of experience of pitches in over 30 countries!! Guess I've seen most of the mistakes – as well as some brilliant winning efforts.

Some summary thoughts:

Nearly all pitches are won, not lost. It's like sport. When we win, we want to believe we have played brilliantly. When we lose… it's because of a refereeing decision, the absence of a key team member through injury, an aberration in the defense. Whatever. But it usually isn't that. It's generally because the opposition played better.

A pitch (a proper pitch) is a process, not one two hour session, and losing agencies have frequently made mistakes early on and compounded them.

Pitches that rely on agencies providing £100,000+ of free creative are a lottery (average cost per agency of a major pitch in the UK £178,000 in 2010), and often agencies win and lose through entirely subjective client decisions. That's why I don't run those pitches any more. Either the client pays, or we use different selection criteria.

Most culpable mistakes? Not rehearsing. Running out of time. Not using a pitch doctor to give a frank view of what the presentation looks like to an outsider. Poor casting. Lying about some aspect of the agency's capability or track record. Cultural errors (especially by US or UK- run international agencies in developing markets).

CONCLUSION

Congratulations. Congratulations. Redux.

Congratulations if you've made it this far.

Yes, I am going to repeat myself. And, I am going to repeat what the industry experts had to say. This is for anyone who, like me, suffers from Ad-Agency-A-D-H-D (AAADHD, take that AAAA's) and also those who might have have skipped to this chapter.

Therefore, I offer a list of the most salient recommendations made in this book.

Agree with me that a well-managed pitch will win you more business.

Take the Go Quiz to make sure that your pitch is worth the effort.

Learn from my "Worst Pitch Ever" story. Beating baby seals is a no-no.

Don't commit agency suicide by making any of the "12 Deadliest Presentation Mistakes".

Use the *Pitch Playbook* management forms that are on my website.

Take the time to really read and dissect the client's pitch documents before you do anything.

Use the Levitan Pitch System and its thirty elements in the sections on Process, Content, Presentation Prep, and Delivery.

Remember that the pitch is really about the client, not your agency.

Work to develop and manage chemistry. Yes, another point I must repeat.

WOW!'s, Chutzpah and BHAGS win pitches.

Absorb the insights and advice from my fourteen Expert Interviews.

Listen hard to the sixteen agency search consultants. Most of them have sat through hundreds of agency presentations and have seen and heard it all.

Last point. Visit my website for up-to-date thoughts and interviews on the subject of agency business development and pitching.

www.peterlevitan.com

Thank you for buying this book. I am sure it will help you win more pitches.

If you have any questions or a great pitch story, give me a shout.

peter@peterlevitan.com

APPENDICES

1. The Industry Speaks On IP

The American Association of Advertising Agencies has addressed the hot topic of who owns the intellectual property presented in a new business pitch. A letter from the 4A's to new business pitch consultants in 2010 urged them to use contract language "that reflects advertising agencies" right to retain creative ideas presented during new-business pitches."

I've reprinted the letter below.

February 2, 2010

4A's New Business Committee Request

Dear Agency Search Consultant:

I am writing to you on behalf of members of the 4A's new business committees. We are reaching out to you because of your involvement with agency search and selection and your interest in fostering mutually beneficial advertiser-agency relationships.

Members of the 4A's new business committees would like to encourage you to consider including a stipulation in all of your agency search agreements that specifies that the rights to Intellectual Property (IP) created by agencies during the review process remain the property of the agency until the marketer either hires the agency to execute the work or the parties agree to a commercially equitable payment for the assignment of usage rights.

In the past the Association has provided background information pertaining to agency new business ownership and usage rights dynamics. The Association has also constructed guidance materials and illustrative contract provisions that equitably address both agency and marketer agency search IP considerations. For your convenience we have included access to some of this material as part of this correspondence (links are provided below). This information is provided for your consideration and use.

Best Practice Guidance: Ownership of Agency Ideas, Plans and Work Developed During The New-Business Process

While the matter is one to be decided by agencies acting individually, the 4A's recommends that agencies preserve ownership of new business-search ideas, plans and work product.

Best Practice Guidance: Agency Search Agreements

The 4A's recommends that agencies execute new business agreements with client prospects at the outset of every agency search.

4A's new business committee members are reaching out to you at this time because the dynamics of agency search-new business are rapidly evolving: Agency-client relationships are shorter in duration. There is increased pressure on agency compensation. Clients are often retaining multiple agencies to execute marketing programs across a proliferating number of media channels. There are more reviews. There are more reviews that request some form of speculative agency work. Because of the economics associated with changing industry dynamics the importance of equitably structuring agency developed new business IP has become more compelling.

Committee members believe that the best interests of all constituents in the marketing community will be well served by adherence to clear equitable agreement on new business IP. We seek your help in eliminating the practice of including ownership assignment provisions in non-disclosure agreements and requiring agencies to assign rights to the agency's work product as a pre-condition to participating in a review. Members of the 4A's new business committees are reaching out to you at this time because you are a thought leader in our industry and you actively participate in the dialog on critical industry economic and relationships matters.

The agencies referenced in the appendix to this letter believe in principle that it is imprudent and inequitable to participate in reviews that require the assignment of agency developed new business ideas and work product. These committee members understand that there are inherent risks and resource investments that are required in the process of their agency's business development. These agencies understand that when new business ideation or speculative work product is included as an agency search mechanism it can help the parties assess capabilities and compatibility. However, the inclusion of new business ideation or speculative work product as a review evaluation mechanism should not include conveyance of valuable intellectual property under commercially unreasonable terms.

Members of the committees respectfully request that you review your agency search agreements and consider, as a matter of principle, advocating agency search agreements specifying that the rights to Intellectual Property (IP) created by agencies during the review process remain the property of the agency until the marketer either hires the agency to execute the work or the parties agree to a commercially equitable payment for the assignment of usage rights.

Thank you for your consideration and ongoing interest in fostering industry beneficial collaboration.

————

2. The Levitan Pitch Playbook

The Levitan Pitch Playbook is on the www.peterlevitan.com website. It includes some pitch management forms that I view as thought starters and guidance to help you manage your pitch.

The Playbook includes:

The Go Quiz

A sample Pitch Creative Brief

A sample agency pitch SWOT analysis and competitive matrix

A Pitch Checklist

A Pitch Budget

A list of chemistry development tools

A one-pager of the 12 Mistakes cartoon in a format suitable for framing

A list of my favorite pitch and presentation books

A list of industry websites that will help you build winning pitches

I will be updating the Playbook as agency pitch life and business development thought leadership moves on. Please let me know if I should include anything that might be of help.

ACKNOWLEDGEMENTS

Many thanks go to my editor Mary Lee, cover designer Ed Hepburn and book designer Andrew Maudlin (this is our second book).

Ridiculously huge thanks go to the very funny Steve Klinetobe of The Cartoon Agency for his advertising pitch mistakes cartoon series.

Stupendous thanks go to all of my expert co-conspirators who helped me get way past having this book be just one man's perspective.

Vasily Ananin

Laura Bajkowski

Paul Bainsfair

Ian Beavis

Robin Boehler

Pete Bogda

Lisa Colantuono

Peter Cowie

Angus Crowther

Joanne Davis

Mike Drexler

Nancy Duarte

Bill Duggan

Marty Finkle

Tom Finneran

Frank Grady

Jerry Gibbons

Bob Hoffman

Michael Jeary

Tony Mikes

Debbie Morrison

Michael Mosynski

Dan Pearlman

Stuart Pocock

Brain Sparks

Sharon Toerek

Russel Wholwerth

Joan Weinberg

Debra Weekley

David Wethy

Darren Woolley

Faris Yakob

Finally, huge thanks to Doug Zanger and his mellifluous voice. He brings this book to life in its audio version.

www.peterlevitan.com

ABOUT THE AUTHOR

Peter Levitan is a serial new business pitcher and has delivered global, regional, and very local new business pitches for over 30 years. He has a Hall Of Fame pitch batting average.

Peter ran business development and marketing at Saatchi & Saatchi Advertising Worldwide in New York and London, and bought and sold three of his own agencies (including Portland's Citrus). He went all-in digital in 1995 to launch online news websites for Advance Publications and founded ActiveBuddy, a natural language technology company that was purchased by Microsoft.

In addition to *"The Levitan Pitch"*, Peter wrote 2012's *"Boomercide: From Woodstock To Suicide"* which offers unique financial planning advice for agency owners after they sell their agency.

Peter runs Peter Levitan & Co., an international advertising agency new business consultancy. He writes and speaks about the art of business development for his blog, industry publications, and events.

16093050R00151

Made in the USA
Middletown, DE
04 December 2014